"*Free Your Mind* goes beyond today's
ment by *using* our thinking, rather
carefully shows us how to use our
conditioning and become truly free

—FRANZ METCALF, Author, *What Would Buddha Do?*

SEP 11 2015
CENTRAL LIBRARY
905-884-9288

"An intelligent book with many concrete examples and unique
perspectives on the internal development on the road to freedom,
that will be helpful for anyone on a spiritual path."

—ANNABELLE ZINSER, Author, *Small Bites: Mindfulness for Everyday Use*

"*Free Your Mind* offers an interesting set of guidelines for exploring
and understanding the nature and potentials of your mind."

—JOEL LEVEY, Author, *Living in Balance: A Mindful Guide for Thriving
in a Complex World*

"Ajay Kapoor's new book, *Free Your Mind*, is both a good read and
a practical tool for those who are new to meditation. And it offers
insights for the more seasoned meditator as well."

—GLENN MULLIN, Author, *The Sacred Sites of the Dalai Lamas*

"*Free Your Mind* is a clever and insightful book that deftly dodges traps
of philosophy, and instead guides the reader directly into their own
experience. Ajay Kapoor lays out the book in a beautifully linear,
accessible manner, so that the reader is taken by the hand and led,
with care and clarity, to the very heart of their own Awakened Mind."

—KEITH MARTIN-SMITH, Author, *A Heart Blown Open*

"Ajay is a humble man with a wealth of knowledge, love, and compassion. His teachings and wisdom have touched and changed many
lives forever, including my own."

— NORA BENO

"Reading Ajay's book has truly changed my life. The teachings are
practical, accessible, and life-altering tools, and offer peace and
truth using a method to help discover our natural state of freedom
simply by examining and shifting the perspective of our thoughts."

— CHRISTINA BRADFORD

BOOK SOLD
NO LONGER R. H P. L.
PROPERTY

DEDICATION

*The life of the author
is dedicated to the Self.*

AJAY KAPOOR

Free Your Mind

A MEDITATION GUIDE TO
Freedom & Happiness

DIVINE
ARTS

Published by DIVINE ARTS
DivineArtsMedia.com

An imprint of Michael Wiese Productions
12400 Ventura Blvd. #1111
Studio City, CA 91604
(818) 379-8799, (818) 986-3408 (FAX)

Cover design: Johnny Ink
Book Layout: William Morosi
Editor: Gary Sunshine
Printed by McNaughton & Gunn, Inc., Saline, Michigan

Manufactured in the United States of America
Copyright 2015 by Ajay Kapoor
All rights reserved. No part of this book may be reproduced in any form or by any means without
permission in writing from the author, except for the inclusion of brief quotations in a review.

Printed on Recycled Stock

CONTENTS

INTRODUCTION

1. This book is not an invention. It is just a recap of the Eternal Principles that govern the human mind. It states in a concise manner how to be happily fulfilled.

2. These Eternal Principles revealed themselves again in the meditations of the author who was just a seer.

3. When you will understand and practice these principles, you will start appreciating and accepting a way of life that is filled with:

   a. Unconditioned Peace
   b. Detachment from desires and expectations
   c. Freedom from all wrong notions and conditionings
   d. Living in total harmony with the Truth
   e. Unconditioned love for one and all

4. This book has been received and presented in a manner that is suited to those who would not like to follow anything without clear understanding. It is written for a mind for which anything abstruse is unattractive and if it is simple and truthful, it is worth embracing.

5. If there is disagreement on anything written in this book, ask questions and proceed further only when your doubts disappear. Make use of email to contact the author (see page 204).

6. This work of deconditioning has been named Z Meditation. "Z" denotes the highest possibility for a human being and "Meditation" means detachment from the mind and realizing a state of unconditioned peace, love, and freedom.

7. Please do not try to "finish" the book. The best way to read it is through simultaneous contemplation and assimilation. Each point and each chapter need to be fully digested before you move on to the next ones.

Purpose of Meditation

Coming Home

The highest possibility for a human being is to live in unconditioned happiness and love. But when you look around, you see that almost everybody is living quite far away from this pristine state of being. The vision of Z Meditation is to bring those who are sincere and willing back home. Those who have gone away from themselves, but want to come back to their inner center, may need compassionate guidance and tools to be able to do so. Z Meditation has been serving this cause since 1997.

Coming home is possible by gaining and practicing right knowledge. It also requires letting go of the wrong knowledge. If you believe you are seeing a snake while you are looking at a rope, you get scared. In reality, you are getting scared because of your wrong vision. The snake is not there. You are only imagining that it is there. In order to get rid of your fear, it is necessary that you give up your illusion and acquire right understanding. As soon as the imaginary snake disappears, you will be peaceful.

You don't need to do anything else. Yes, for attaining freedom from your mental turmoil, you don't need to do anything else. You only need to do deep contemplation and get rid of wrong notions. You only need to gain right knowledge and practice it sincerely. Doing this, you shall obtain freedom from all fears and insecurities. You will naturally become peaceful and happy. There is no need to do any difficult yogic postures! There is no need to do any esoteric mantras. There is no need to do even those difficult visualizations. All these exercises that are taught in the name of meditation are just the initial preparatory warm-ups to gain stability. They are helpful for the beginners. But they don't change the understanding of the practitioner. The evolution of the understanding is a different game altogether. *Transformation and Upliftment of the Perspective is The Way. Letting go of the illusions is the straightest Path.* In the end, we will understand that the true purpose of meditation is to elevate the mind to its highest possibility of unconditioned peace and love. We will not only understand — we will experience this state as our most natural state of being.

There are various rungs that a meditator must climb in this process. It begins with **studying or listening** to the right knowledge. The test of rightness is that it should be verifiable by one and all. If it is not and if things appear to be mysterious, there could be something wrong or very ordinary. The highest knowledge is very, very simple and easy to grasp. There is nothing esoteric about it.

Secondly, after having listened to the Truth, one needs to **deeply contemplate** upon it. When one does that, it gets **integrated** with one's life. The speed of progress depends upon the sincerity of the seeker. If spiritual growth becomes one's topmost priority in life, the destination can be reached very rapidly. We have seen people experiencing the higher states of consciousness within a few days of the work.

These are the three steps in Z Meditation practice:

1. Freedom from wrong notions, conditionings, and the resultant suffering: Deep Deconditioning Inquiry is employed for this purpose. This book will teach the theory of meditation and six questions of Deep Deconditioning Inquiry.

2. Establishment in right understanding, unconditioned happiness, and love: Six Radiant Mantras are learned and these Mantras help us fully live in the moment.

3. Experiencing the Eternal Blissful Awareness as one's true identity: as the Inquiry deepens further in the third level, one reaches this sublime state of eternal freedom.

The learning and practice of Z Meditation happens in this order only. Unless you free yourself from your illusions, you cannot be peaceful. If you are not peaceful, your happiness cannot be stable. If you are not happy, your mind will keep running after the objects that you believe will give you happiness. With this restless mind, you cannot meditate and experience Eternal Blissful Awareness as your true identity.

In this book, you will first gain the understanding of the functioning of your mind. After that, the philosophy and practice of meditation will be taught in a progressive way so that even beginners will be able to grasp this subtle knowledge easily. Toward the end, you will learn the six questions of Deep Deconditioning Inquiry that will help you uncover the deepest conditionings in your mind.

We hope that our journey together will be full of love and joy.

FIVE PRINCIPLES OF
Z MEDITATION

There are five basic premises that make the backbone of Z Meditation:

NO PROOF, NO BELIEF

All beliefs should be experientially verifiable by one and all. That is, everybody should be able to experience the truth hidden in the beliefs. If experience is not possible, then they could just be random figments of the imagination of creative minds.

NO CONCEPTS, NO PEACE

There is zero possibility of *suppressing* the turbulence of the mind by mechanical means. For attaining lasting peace, the concepts about the mind's design and its source must be clearly understood.

NO MOTHER-TONGUE, NO UNDERSTANDING

One best understands in one's own language. Without understanding, one cannot integrate this knowledge with one's real life. Using a language that one does not understand makes concepts unnecessarily difficult to grasp.

No Tuning, No Music

Meditation cannot happen if one's practice consists of hard austerities in which one tortures the body or the mind. The work on the mind ought to be an enjoyable and radiant way to clear it of its turmoil. Meditation makes one see things in the Light of Truth. If one is practicing self-affliction and torture, one cannot think clearly. Without clear thinking, one cannot detach from one's age-old conditionings.

Middle path is the best path. Moderation in eating, sleeping, and recreation is undoubtedly helpful for meditation.

No Integration, No Dance

Meditation is a way of life and not just a routine practice. If the rest of the day is not lived in conformity with what one practices in one's meditation, one can be termed a hypocrite. One must integrate the concepts with one's real life. Also, one cannot make progress just by doing some monotonous and mechanical exercises. One should assimilate the concepts about absolute truths.

These are revolutionary principles of meditation. Integrating them with one's practice, one can make speedy and steady progress in this beautiful mind-elevation game.

OBJECTIVES OF THE BOOK

1. To recognize and remove all the illusions of understanding.

2. To experientially understand the difference between dreaming and living in reality.

3. To develop a skill for removing the mental clutter.

4. To develop an expertise of filtering the feelings from this clutter.

5. To understand the functioning of the mind — your own as well as those of people around you — and gain awareness about the *Causal Platforms* from where people operate. Once you have the knowledge about these platforms, you learn to remain balanced even in the most difficult interpersonal situations.

6. To understand and appreciate why most people are not peaceful and learn to apply the Laws of Peace in one's own life.

7. To understand and experience the real meaning of freedom, which is nothing but detachment from all wrong conditionings.

8. To understand the damaging effects of interfering in others' business and to get trained in living in one's own real business.

9. To know what it means and takes to live in the Here and Now.

In short, you are going to learn to use a unique tool called Deep Deconditioning Inquiry that will help you get detached from your conditionings and restlessness. You will find yourself very well equipped to face all challenges in life. Living in a state of unconditioned peace and love will become spontaneous and effortless.

Some Useful Hints for Studying This Book

1. This is a book for learning how to do profound contemplation for spiritual growth. You will learn how to detach yourself from your mental turmoil and do Deep Deconditioning Inquiry. The Inquiry will elevate your mind to the state of freedom in no time.

2. Each chapter is written in the form of meditative points. Study one point. Stop and contemplate. Integrate it with your mindset. Digest it well and then move forward.

3. When you go to your place of work, apply the concepts there. Meditation ought not to finish on the meditation seat. It is a way of life.

4. In the evening, do the revision. Sit down again to contemplate. See for yourself if you lived up to the principles or not. Ask yourself: "What more can I do?"

5. There are many true stories used in the book to help you understand the process of Deep Inquiry. The names of people have been changed to respect privacy.

6. If you find terseness anywhere, it is a deliberate attempt to make you contemplate. Try to bridge the gaps on your own. If you have doubts or need clarifications, please send an email to the author.

Thinking vs. Dreaming

*In order to have good meditation,
snap yourself out of daydreams.*

1. For knowing the current state of your mind, do
   a simple exercise. Keep a pen and notebook
   with you. Sit straight and focus on your breath.
   When you inhale, in your mind, say "Om."
   On exhaling, do reverse counting from one
   hundred — one count with each breath. If, on
   the way down, some thoughts disturb you, note
   them down and start all over again. Do this for
   half an hour and after that, move on to the
   next page.

2. After half an hour, study yourself in your notebook. You might have written tens of thoughts. You might also have forgotten so many others. You will see that most of the thoughts are incoherent and futile. You will also appreciate that most of the time, you remained *lost* in these thoughts and you could not have a smooth flow of concentration.

3. The "Om" and counting thoughts are your intentional and voluntary thoughts. They represent **thinking.** You can call them **thinking thoughts**.

4. All the other thoughts are *coming* to you involuntarily and unintentionally. Do you realize that most of the time, you remain drowned in this ocean of unconscious thoughts? These thoughts are random, uncontrolled, and disjointed. You may call them **dream thoughts** — as they make all our daydreams. We also call them **thoughting**.

5. There are certain properties of a restless mind that is always lost in dream thoughts:

   a. Extreme restlessness — daydreaming most the time.

b. Lack of mindfulness while doing
daily activities.

c. Dissatisfaction with the present situation
in life. There is also a strong desire to
control the future or change the past.

d. Due to this dissatisfaction, worrying
about the future or regretting the past.

6. **It is *either* the thinking *or* the dream
thoughts that can occupy the mind *at a time.***
You cannot dream and also be aware at the
same time.

7. **The current state of restlessness is not accidental.** You are unconsciously choosing your
dream thoughts. Please think why you don't
get an involuntary thought about the president of U.S. and why most of your thoughts
are either about your close friends and relatives or the current situation you are caught
up with.

8. **Thinking or dreaming — make a choice.**
You can become a master of your mind by
learning to choose which thoughts to have
and which not. Yes, it is possible to have
such control over your thinking. The first
step in this direction is to invoke a strong
desire that there is nothing more important
in life than gaining mastery over oneself.

ILLUSION OF DUALITY

You just experience yourself all the time.

John Mayor, a resident of San Francisco, had to go to New York for some office work. His wife, Nancy, wanted to accompany him as she was a little suspicious about his behavior over the last few days. He had been regularly coming back late. John was not happy with the idea of Nancy going to New York with him. He hated this unnecessary fuss that her senseless suspicion was creating. They had a big fight over this issue and John left the house in disgust. He was now planning to file for divorce.

1. The whole episode lasted for only fifteen minutes. Thank God, it was just a bad dream! John got up and saw the time. It was 3 a.m. He smiled and looked at Nancy who was snoring gently. He decided to go to his meditation room and reflect over the dream.

2. John understood that it was just his mind's play. It was his own mind that had assumed various names and forms in the dream. There was nothing that had happened in reality. He himself had become San Francisco, New York, Nancy, commotion, thoughts about divorce, etc. He himself had also become all the feelings like disgust and anger.

Everything was his mind's creation. In the dream state, the subject of the dream, John Mayor, and all the objects experienced, were coming from the same source — him. He was experiencing just his own mental formations.

3. When he woke up, the knower of the dream was also he himself.

4. As John was contemplating, he asked himself some questions: Just like the dreams at night, am I not lost in daydreams during the day too? What is it that I experience when I am daydreaming? Is it not that I am becoming my dreams and when I am lost in them, I mistakenly consider them to be reality? Was my suffering in that night dream justified? What is it that I suffered about? Is my suffering during daytime justified? What is it that I suffer about?

5. When you are lost in the dream state, you wrongly believe that you are experiencing many distinct objects or people that have identities separate from your own. Actually, you experience only yourself. You just have *the illusion of duality*. The objects of your dream have no identity apart from you. The subject and objects are one and even the knower in the waking state is the same — YOU.

ILLUSION OF REALITY

While you are dreaming, you are invariably lost.
You unconsciously believe the dream to be reality.

1. Think about this question for a while: "In
   the dream state, when John was arguing with
   his wife, could he do anything different?"
   Could he choose to remain considerate
   and compassionate?

2. Actually, this question is absurd as we cannot
   ever know that we are dreaming while the
   dream is going on. **It is only on waking up that
   our perception changes** and we come to a position of understanding and analyzing.

3. On waking up, John understood that while the
   dream was going on, he was unaware that it was
   a dream. **During that period of dreaming, he
   was wrongly considering the experience to be
   real.** That is why he was feeling unhappy and
   stressed. **This is the illusion of reality.**

4. In the waking state of consciousness, when we
   are apparently awake but actually dreaming,
   what is it that we experience? Is it not our own
   mental formations, there also?

5. The substance of at least 95% of our experiences is our own imaginations because we
   spend all this time of our lives dreaming!
   We are so lost in dreams that there hardly
   occurs a moment when we come out and
   are objective about them. Unless we can
   be objective about our own mental formations, we cannot do any uplifting work on
   the mind.

6. All our suffering is happening in dreams
   only! **When there is awareness, there cannot
   be suffering**. When John is awake, is he still
   suffering because Nancy was suspicious in
   the dream?

7. **When dream thoughts are there, one's
   awareness sleeps and when awareness
   awakens, dreaming disappears.**

8. In order to have awareness, which is a
   necessary prerequisite for meditation, we
   need to learn to snap ourselves out of our
   daydreams.

ILLUSION OF INCOMPLETENESS

"I + X = C" is an illusion.

1. All of us wish to achieve a state of completeness and fulfillment. Nobody wants to be incomplete or dissatisfied. It is only when this state of inner wholeness is experienced that one can be truly happy.

2. However, our experience is just the opposite. Despite an ingrained desire to be complete and happy, we are dissatisfied and unhappy, most of the time.

3. Is incompleteness real or imaginary? Please think about this.

4. Contemplate upon and write down your definitions of reality and imagination.

5. This incompleteness is imaginary. There are two imaginary equations of incompleteness that we believe in:

   $I + X = C$

   $I - X = IC$

   That is:

   Myself + an external factor = a state of completeness

Myself – an external factor = a state of incompleteness

These equations mean that we feel a desire for some external factor(s) to be complete and happy. The X in these equations can be money, people, a situation, an environment, a job, a place, time, etc. We believe that there is something incomplete in us and we will remove it with the fulfillment of our desires related to our X factors.

6. If these equations were true, how could these facts be explained:

   a. The same X giving happiness now and unhappiness at another time, i.e., happiness diminishing with time.

   b. The same X giving happiness to one and unhappiness to another at the same time.

7. "I + X = C" is absolutely untrue. It creates an *imaginary* void in the mind. One then starts living in a chase mode to fill up that void.

8. Even when the void is temporarily filled up, the unconscious understanding that "there must be something or somebody to depend upon" is not given up. One just keeps running from one object to another all the time.

WHERE DO WE EXPERIENCE HAPPINESS?

When the mind is restful,
peace, well-being, and happiness are experienced.

When the mind is restless,
pleasure, excitement, or unhappiness is experienced.

One elderly lady was searching for her lost needle under a pole of light on her street. She could not find it anywhere. One gentleman came and asked her if he could be of some help to her. She explained the situation and now the two of them were searching for the lost needle. One hour passed and they could not find it anywhere. Then a wise lady came and offered her help. She asked the elderly lady where she had dropped the needle. The elderly lady said that she had dropped it somewhere in her room! The wise lady asked her why was she searching for it outside the room, in the street? The elderly lady said she was doing it because there was no light in her room and there was light on the street!

1. Isn't it absurd? Isn't it unintelligent? Isn't it stupid, this kind of behavior? Can such a search ever bear fruit?

2. Similarly, the search for happiness will be fruitful only when we look for it where we have lost it. *Happiness is a state of one's own mind.* One cannot

find it anywhere outside of oneself. People try to find it in their various X factors. It does not exist in any X factor. That is why most of us on this planet are unhappy.

3. *Happiness is not a transportable or transferable entity.* Money cannot give it to you. Relatives cannot give it to you. Friends cannot give it to you. You only imagine that it comes from them and you start *acting* and *reacting* accordingly. Nothing is being exchanged in reality — you are only living in your false imaginations!

4. There is a spiritual truth: *When the mind is restful, peace and happiness are experienced. When the mind is restless, temporary pleasure or unhappiness is experienced.* The actual question is: What is our true requirement — a restful and happy mind or a restless and unhappy mind?

5. If your car needs overhauling and you start renovating your house, will it ever help your car? If entity A needs repair, you cannot be working on entity B instead. *If you want to be happy, it is the mind that needs to be fixed.* Just fixing the external circumstances is not going to serve this purpose. Your accumulation of wealth or your chasing people is not going to be of any avail. Have you not tried it enough yet?

ILLUSION OF PERMANENCE

Which desire leads to lasting fulfillment?

There was a bull living in a village in India. It used to plow the lands of a poor farmer who would make it slog day in and day out. One day, it prayed to God that it wanted to exchange roles with its master. God listened and immediately fulfilled the bull's desire. Now, the bull-farmer had to take care of the family. It was a big responsibility. His wife was very nagging and demanding. The children were cranky and he also had to manage the ruffian landlord of the village. The bull-farmer got fed up in only seven days and started praying to God to make him the landlord of the village. And God fulfilled this desire also.

As the landlord of the village, the responsibilities grew further. He had to report to the king every week and pay him a lot of money to keep him happy. The king was cruel and would kill anybody even for a trivial reason. The bull-landlord got exhausted here also and started praying to God to make him the king. God fulfilled this wish also and made him the king.

The kingship also lasted for only a few days as the responsibilities and headaches grew further. In the end, the bull-king prayed to God to give back to him the peaceful life of a bull!

1. When you believe that you need something or somebody or some change in life to be happy, how do you feel during that period of inadequacy? Do you feel happy?

2. And when the desire gets fulfilled, how long does your happiness last?

3. When you are caught up in a desire, do you understand that the result will be temporary and you will be hopping on to something else in a few days? Do you remember that you were dying for another X factor, just a few days back?

4. This understanding that happiness will come from somewhere else is at the root of all suffering. It never comes and you keep chasing.

5. Most of us are infected with the illusion of permanence also — if this desire gets fulfilled, it will give me lasting happiness or it will be the end of all my problems! What actually happens is that when one desire gets fulfilled, you start taking it for granted and then you create new desires as the fulfillment of the previous one did not give you lasting happiness. It remains like that forever. You keep forgetting that even

the last time when your desire got fulfilled, nothing much had changed in you.

6. Each solution we seek tends to become the seed of some new problems in life. It is an endless cycle.

It-Will-Be-Better-Elsewhere Mindset

You cannot be happy in the future or past.
Happiness always happens in the present.

Susan Claire was in the office taking dictation from her boss, Tom. It was 9:30 in the morning and she was already exhausted. She had been living in a strong dilemma about her job. She wanted to discontinue this work. She strongly desired to go back to school to get her degree in elementary education. She loved children and wanted to take up teaching as her profession. She believed that she would be happy only in the future when things would change.

As she came out of Tom's room and went to her cubicle, she was on the verge of crying: "How long? How long will it continue?"

Susan felt helpless. She could not give up the job as there were many urgent responsibilities on her shoulders. She kept brooding throughout the day, but could not come up with any clear decision.

This state of indecision continued for years.

1. Is this not the mindset of most of us? Is a Susan living in you too?

2. What are the essential properties of this kind of a mind?

a. Inability to enjoy the present moment.

b. Daydreaming most of the time, if not all the time.

c. Desire to change the current circumstances that appear to be heavy to bear. There is a constant hope that when things will change, only then will there be happiness in life.

d. Worrying about the future or regretting the past.

e. Helplessness and restlessness.

f. Running in circles.

g. Lack of awareness and fickleness.

3. By remaining perpetually dissatisfied with the present, one invariably spoils one's life. Do you see another possibility in which Susan can accept the present and yet do her best to follow the course of her calling with peace in her heart? Can one be balanced and passionate at the same time? Can attachment and detachment exist simultaneously in a mind?

4. If life does not allow Susan to become a teacher, can she still be peaceful and fulfilled? If you were in Susan's position, what would you do? And why?

UTILITY STANDPOINT

Running in circles never takes you to your goal.
Thoughtfulness may.

Enat had her final exams going on. She had come to the U.S. and got accepted to Stanford to pursue her MBA. She had been studying hard for her exams. But today, it was extremely difficult to concentrate. She was missing her parents who lived in Tel Aviv. She got a call from her mother in the morning. Her mother was not well and she wanted Enat to come back to Israel immediately.

Enat sat in front of her textbook for three hours and she had not turned even a single page. She was continuously revolving around "Should I go back; should I not...."

1. In the background of most of our minds, unconscious and futile daydreaming continuously goes on. When such daydreaming is happening, one mistakenly takes it to be reality and, therefore, one does not remain aware of the reality of the moment. When one is not aware, one's efficiency in the moment reduces considerably. What one could have achieved in less time and with less effort, one takes much more time and effort to do.

2. Enat is, in reality, not moving an inch further toward what she is concerned about. She is only doing circles in her mind. She is neither deciding about going back nor studying. She is just confused.

3. The ideal scenario is: jot down the pros and cons of each solution and make a decision, keeping your priorities straight. Whether Enat should go back or not is not the question. The question is: "Why should she go or why should she not go?" She has to see what is truly important for her and then arrive at a clear decision. Merely remaining lost is never a solution to any problem.

4. So even from a utilitarian standpoint — letting fulfillment of desire be the criterion of utility — living in daydreams or running in circles is not a solution to any problem.

5. One can only take the best possible thoughtful steps in the right direction of the future. All the rest is a waste of energies.

REBECCA-MIND AND HAPPINESS

*One cannot not live in the present moment
and be peacefully happy also.*

*Rebecca was married to Paul for thirty years. Although they had spent
many happy times together, she always carried this grudge in her
heart: "Why doesn't he have words of appreciation for me? Why does
Paul appear indifferent at times and even callous, sometimes? With
everybody else, he is quite positive and loving, but with me, there's
something missing... "*

1. A Rebecca-mind is considered *normal* even by
   our psychologists! In this mind, the background
   is noisy and is full of expectations and desires
   from others. *These expectations and desires are
   considered natural by most people in our world.*

2. A Rebecca-mind has these basic qualities of
   grasping and rejection: She tries to grasp
   success, gain, praise, and love. She naturally
   rejects failure, loss, blame, and the possibility of
   her love not getting reciprocated. She grasps in
   the hope of happiness. She rejects in the hope
   of happiness. The consequence is suffering,
   which can be in the form of sadness, worries,
   stress, depression, hopelessness, jealousy, anger,

restlessness, boredom, loneliness, dejection, fears, or any such unhappy feeling.

3. Even when this mind appears to be happy sometimes, there are these shortcomings:

   a. There is a lack of control over the mind as it keeps dreaming.

   b. There is no awareness of the present moment and it still lives in the past or future.

   c. The seeds of grasping and rejection remain hidden in the unconscious base of the mind. This gives birth to insecurity and fears about the future.

4. Imagine a state in which grasping and rejection have vanished. What would the experience be like? Surely, an experience of unconditioned peace and happiness will take place.

5. An important question for a Rebecca is: Do you really want grasping and rejection more than peace and happiness? Because of their ignorance that X factors always lead to suffering, many Rebeccas remain trapped in their restlessness. Given right under-standing, at least some of them will happily fly out of the clutches of their minds.

FOR OR FROM?

"$I = C$"

Michel was a publisher of IT books and was quite successful in this field. His employees were very smart and would always keep him ahead of other competitors. He would also take good care of the entire company.

After working hard for fifteen years, Michel started feeling burnt out. Something was missing in his life. He could not exactly figure out what it was, but he was dissatisfied. He tried to take the help of a counselor, but it did not work.

Then Michel went to India where he met a monk in the Himalayas. He stayed with the monk for three months and learned the art of deconditioning the mind to realize its true nature. As he had a sincere and subtle mind, his practice deepened and after about a year of living in India, he went back to Sydney to publish the IT books again!

He lived happily thereafter and helped a lot of people as well!

  1. There are only two ways of living in this world:

     a. Living *for* completeness: $I + X = C$.

     b. Living *from* completeness: $I = C$.

In the first part of his life, Michel was living a good life. He had a successful business, a nice wife, beautiful children, and a daily list of chores. But, he had little awareness about how his mind operated. It just followed the customary ways of living — believing that happiness comes from X factors. Eventually, in such cases, if the mind is subtle enough, exhaustion and meaninglessness ensue.

In the second part, when he became aware of the mind and the conditionings that drive it, he started a process of disillusionment through meditation. Then the entire perspective of living changed. The same job, the same people around, the same chores — but he was now in total control of his thoughts. The fulfillment no longer depended upon the externals. He was now a free man. He was now a happy man.

The second kind of life is for a very few brave ones who dare to walk the virgin lands. *The illusion that happiness comes from outside is the only obstacle.* In this second scenario, the X factory is dropped and the greatest fulfillment of "I = C" is experienced!

Dharma

What is your best possibility?

1. This question is often asked in the Z Meditation retreats: "Now that I have learned that I just need to work on myself and realize a state of inner completeness, what next? I accept this life in which I live from completeness and not for; but what to do after that?"

2. It is very simple, now onward. Once you let go of the illusions of duality, reality, permanence, and incompleteness, once your X factors are dropped and you realize that your fulfillment is already within you, you just have to let your *dharma* shine forth. Dharma in this context means *your natural state of being.* It might be physics for an Einstein, painting for a Picasso, or writing for a Tagore. It could be social service for a Mother Teresa, religion for a Dalai Lama, or soccer for a Pelé. You just need to love your dharma and fill up your time following it.

3. That means you are not dependent upon the results of your actions anymore. *You follow your dharma with love, happiness, and awareness. You don't*

want to win games; you just love playing. The pairs of opposites — success-failure, gain-loss, praise-blame etc. — are inconsequential for you.

4. You need to differentiate very thoughtfully between *giving your life a meaningful dharmic direction* and *doing things for some distant fruits.* The latter gives worries. The former is a joyful process. While following your passion, you will still need to draw strategies; you will still be busy. But you will not be anxious or stressed about the results of what you do. For you, the means will be the goals.

5. There will of course be problems on the way. But for you, solving them will be like solving sums of mathematics. You will do that with equanimity and joy. You will take on things as and when they present them-selves to you. You will never have any reason to hurry or worry.

6. Keeping the X factors alive in your life simply means that you have desires and you believe that their fulfillment will give you fulfillment. It never happens. When you get disillusioned from this basic flaw in under-standing, your entire life becomes a joyful celebration. Each day of your life is lived

with love — love for yourself, love for what you do, and love for people around you.

7. Unconditioned happiness and love are the primary dharmas of all human beings — whether they realize it or not is a different matter altogether. When this primary dharma shines with the renunciation of desires, one's secondary dharma naturally starts glowing. There will be no reason for such a person to follow any vocation other than his true dharma.

THREE QUALITIES OF MIND

Nothing is to be taken personally.
Everybody here is acting compulsively.

1. How is it that some people are greedy and some generous? Some are compassionate and some callous? Some are lazy and some overactive? Some are contemplative and some flippant? How and why are people different from one other?

2. These differences are natural. There are three inherent qualities of the mind: Tamas (Lethargy), Rajas (Sensuality), and Sattwa (Purity or Integrity). As liquidity, transparency, and wetness are to water, as heat and light are to the Sun, these three inherent qualities are to the mind — all human minds.

3. A child does not come out of the womb with a clean mental slate. Its mind has inbuilt properties that manifest with age.

4. The first quality is *Lethargy* with *confusion and chaos* as its main attributes.

5. The second is *Sensuality* with *dependence on sensual objects and endless activities* as its main features.

6. The third is *Purity* with *knowledge and happiness* as its main traits.

7. Everybody has all these three qualities. You cannot find anybody in this world who can say that he has one more or one less.

8. Still, people differ in their behavior. It is because the proportion of the three qualities is different in each one. People can be lethargic, sensual, or pure, depending on the preponderance of the respective quality. It is not that a lethargic person will not have sensuality or purity at all. It is just that he will be predominantly lethargic. And the same with the other two.

9. Let us study the three qualities with three *real* examples.

   a. Sam, the lethargic.
   b. Tom and Sarah, the sensuals.
   c. Mark, the pure.

SAM'S LETHARGIC PATTERNS

Never give uncalled-for advice.
Especially to a congenital whiner.

1. Sam and his wife, Shrutz, live in New Delhi.
   One day, Sam had to pick up his wife at the
   airport. She was coming back from a silent
   meditation retreat of ten days. On their way
   back, they realized that there was no gas in
   their car and they got stuck in the middle of
   a highway. Sam was very unhappy with Shrutz
   because he felt that she should have paid
   more attention and reminded him the day
   before about filling up the tank. He was yelling
   throughout the day, blaming her for what had
   happened. And this was not the first time.

2. Sam and Shrutz went for a picnic with their two
   children. He was driving the car as he knew
   the way to the picnic spot on the beach. It so
   happened that he lost the way and had to drive
   back for about fifteen miles. Shrutz had dozed
   off when this happened. She was woken up by
   her ever-unhappy husband who again blamed
   her that it was because she had slept that they

lost the way. He was now driving back home in anger!

3. Sam needs about twelve hours of sleep every day. In his waking time, he either watches football or chats with his friends on the telephone or the Internet. He runs the household with the income from renting his properties. Shrutz is a makeup artist. Her income and the rental income are barely sufficient for their family, but that is never a concern for Sam.

4. Sam gets very angry if anyone gives him advice — especially Shrutz.

5. Sam has grand plans for earning millions of dollars in a short time. He just keeps living in his fantasies and never does anything about it. If somebody encourages him to get going or tries to bring about a direction in his life, he feels irritated, morose, or angry.

6. If Shrutz asks him to search for a job, he feels that she is his biggest enemy. He sometimes threatens her that he will commit suicide if she keeps pestering him to find a job.

7. If Sam gives an opinion and you support him on that, he can instantly reject it and start advocating a different one. He really

feels from his heart that he knows best and most others are fools — especially Shrutz!

8. When faced with a problem, he gets nervous and looks toward Shrutz to bring him out of the mess he so often creates. After taking her help, he is never grateful. He never acknowledges the fact that some-times others can also be right.

9. When he takes out his clothes from the closet, he spoils the entire stack and does not understand that he is creating unneces-sary trouble for others. It takes Shrutz a lot of time to mend what he does.

10. He often broods and laments that his mother did not allow him to join the army twenty years before. He feels he would have excelled there.

11. Sam does not like discipline. He likes freedom!

12. He does not normally do things on time. He always feels that it can happen better the next day, as he would get more time to think. The next day, he needs some more time to think. It goes on and on. And when he cannot postpone anymore and has to take steps, he does it halfheartedly

as if it is a big load of work that he has to somehow finish.

13. One mostly sees him saying that he does not have time or his life is too busy. In reality, he passes his time gossiping or watching television.

14. When he is sick, he becomes like a child. He needs plenty of attention and care. But when the children or Shrutz are sick, he hardly pays any attention. He is very busy, especially during those times.

15. He is never happy with his neighbors. He feels that they are all selfish and he should always keep his defenses up.

LETHARGY

"Confusion" is from nature, not from individuals.
Why get upset?

Let us study the main traits of Tamas or lethargy:

1. In a lethargic person, confusion reigns supreme
   in the mind. He cannot easily draw inferences
   and conclusions. Given a cause, what could
   be the effect and given an effect, what were
   the possible causes — he cannot think along
   these lines.

2. He mostly remains indecisive. He runs in circles
   of vagueness and triviality. If he has to deal with
   a problem, he cannot think about the possible
   solutions. He just revolves around "I have a
   problem… I have a problem." He cannot weigh
   in terms of pros and cons in any given situation.
   He cannot even try to think about the consequences of his actions.

3. He does not and cannot gauge his potential and
   yet feels great pride in his abilities!

4. His fears and worries are baseless. He could be constantly scared that he would be run over by a car or would get sucked into a black hole!

5. He is fickle-minded to the extreme. Even in a short conversation, you can see him changing his views very quickly.

6. He lives mostly in the past and is mostly unhappy about it. He often has these lethargic feelings of sadness, regret, guilt, jealousy, lamentation, grief, depression, etc. These feelings are putrefying as they don't let him move on with life.

7. He does not have anything to look forward to. That is, he does not have ambitions and goals to achieve. His mind has countless incoherent thoughts and he is always lost in them. There is *no* possibility of his coming out of this jungle.

8. He may have severe mood swings.

9. His room and closet are always disorganized — just like his mind and life.

10. He procrastinates even his important tasks. Today is never a good day for him to take necessary steps.

11. He can be creative in lying and finding excuses. He is irresponsible in his

jobs. His undertakings are unsteady.
His work is shoddy and clearly smells
of thoughtlessness.

12. He is insensitive in relationships. He can be
very callous toward others' feelings.

13. He never owns responsibility. He always
blames, criticizes, and holds others responsible for his unhappiness and failures.

14. He can be foolishly stubborn at times.

15. He despises listening to others. In extreme
cases of lethargy, he also can be malicious,
quarrelsome, abusive, and cruel.

16. He resorts to lazy means to get away from
the chaos of his mind. The X factor of a
lethargic person can be alcohol, drugs,
viewing television for hours at a stretch,
gossiping, oversleeping, etc.

17. It is not just individuals; even nations/
communities can be lethargic. When you
see broken roads not being repaired,
crisscrossing electric wires, corruption and
bribery in administration, shoddy jobs, fruit-
less gossiping, and an inability to accept
positive criticism and advice, you can easily
make out that the people of such places are
predominantly lethargic.

Sarah and Tom's Hectic Lifestyle

Desires and Peace never go together.

1. Tom gets up at six in the morning. He wakes up his children and prepares them for going to school. His wife, Sarah, leaves home earlier. Her work starts at seven. Tom leaves at 7:30. He drives twenty miles to first reach the day care of his two-year-old son. Dropping him there, he goes to his daughter's school and then to his office around 8:30. He gets to work late by a few minutes, almost daily.

2. He leaves the office at 5:25 in the evening and picks up his children. By the time he reaches home, it is seven o'clock. He watches television and plays with his children for some time. He brings home his work that he must finish before going to sleep at 11:00.

3. In the evening, it is Sarah who prepares the dinner. After giving her children their evening shower, she retires around 9:30.

4. The weekends are always packed for both of them. They do shopping, laundry, dishes, and cleaning on Saturdays. On Sundays, they go out either for a party or to a movie. Sometimes, they invite their friends for dinner for which they remain very busy throughout the day.

5. Both Tom and Sarah have many desires from life and from each other. Sarah wants to see her husband become the CEO of a big company.

6. Tom and Sarah want to have a lot of money.

7. They like traveling to exotic locations. In the last ten years, they have changed three houses and three cars.

8. When some desires are fulfilled or when they are enjoying with friends, they are happy. When they are at home, they are neither happy nor unhappy. They just follow their routines.

9. Tom and Sarah have family-oriented minds — everything for their own family only. The outsiders don't form a part of their involuntary thinking. They sometimes visit their parents too.

10. They can go on living this life until they have to finally retire. They look forward to the days when they will be able to relax.

SENSUALITY

They manufacture stress and emptiness in the X factory.

Let us now study Rajas or sensuality:

1. A sensual person feels that the objects of the senses are the only reality; happiness is dependent on sense pleasures; desires must be present and their fulfillment is the goal of life. He feels that "eat, drink, and enjoy" is the best philosophy in life.

2. He believes that to fulfill the desires, one should work hard and one should spend most of one's time in working to earn a lot of money.

3. The X factory of a sensual person consists of money, sex, relationships, power, status, superiority, praise, approval, gadgets, cars, houses, etc.

4. My wife and my children — this is his entire world.

5. If his desires get fulfilled, he celebrates. If there are obstacles on the way, he is sad and restless.

6. His mind is ever insatiable and it always has desire for *more* — more money, bigger car, bigger house, new travel destinations. His life is all about making it big.

7. Clear strategy, perfect planning, and relent-less execution — this is his way. But he does it only for the fulfillment of his desires. He finds it difficult to do anything for the sake of helping others. He is not motivated by the idea of selfless compassion.

8. His inferences and conclusions are clear. He considers positive the manipulations and calculations to reach the desired goals. He loves overtaking others.

9. A sensual person lives mostly in the future and is habitually stressed about it.

10. He places many expectations upon the people around him. However, if others place similar demands upon him, he is not happy.

11. He sometimes gets excited by transient patriotic or philanthropic feelings. But such feelings don't last long. His large-heartedness is as temporary as froth.

12. He has many ambitions and goals, but their fulfillment never gives him lasting fulfillment.

13. He loves to begin new activities as his desires are countless.

14. "Peace and compassion should be practiced when one is old" — he feels.

15. "People who meditate are those who are good for nothing and cannot do anything else" — he thinks.

16. He suffers from stressful feelings like greed, anger, pride, lust, and attachment. These feelings goad him to work more and more.

17. His vacations are spent in exotic locations. It is for temporary relief that he goes to these places. He needs a different place each time.

18. If he ever donates, he does it for recognition or for some other ulterior motive.

19. He likes to eat pungent and hot things. He needs a lot of variety in food. He loves to go to a new restaurant every time he goes out for dinner.

20. Between "pleasant" and "good," he would prefer the former.

21. He cannot wait. He hardly has any patience.

22. He cannot understand that discontentment is not happiness, chasing is not reaching, and stress is not good for his health. He is too busy to have time for his own growth.

MARK WELLHAMS' INTEGRITY

Mindfulness is a prerequisite for fulfillment.

1. Mark lives in Holland. Alone, but never lonely. He works part-time for an NGO that helps seniors. He loves his job and looks forward to going to work every day.

2. His day begins at 5:30 a.m. After his morning ablutions — clearing the bowels is a must for him — he meditates for two hours and tries to experience the state of blissful silence within. Mark believes that unless one clears the mind with meditation in the morning, it is difficult to remain aware and peaceful during the rest of the day. He finishes his meditation with a resolve to carry it to the rest of the day.

3. He understands that unless one lets go of the societal programming, one cannot be peaceful. Being in the state of peace, fulfillment, and love is what he cherishes and guards with utmost care.

4. He leaves at 9:45 for his work. His office is just a ten-minute walk from home. He walks mindfully

to the office and this gives him a good meditative bridge between home and work. From his office, he needs to go to various old-age homes to help the seniors there. He consciously sees to it that he remains calm and compassionate throughout the day.

5. He comes back home at 3:30 in the afternoon. Then he mindfully prepares his lunch and eats it with awareness and gratitude.

6. Mark must take a nap of at least half an hour in the afternoon as he wants to feel fresh for his evening meditation. At five o'clock, he sits for meditation — releasing the futile programs and realizing stillness of the Self. He believes that unless one practices regularly and systematically, it is difficult to get rid of the inner turmoil.

7. He sometimes watches spiritual programs on television and sometimes studies scriptures. This is like tonic for his soul. He does his evening eating meditation with salads and fruits around 9:00. Sometimes, he watches programs on Discovery Channel.

8. Before going to sleep at 11:00, he sits for the last dose of meditation for fifteen minutes. When he is on his back on the

bed, he keeps practicing meditation until he falls asleep.

9. On Saturdays, Mark visits his parents. He also goes to a monastery to meet his community and listen to the discourses. He likes to remain at home on Sundays and just relax, and meditate, and walk, and visit a park to see dogs and children playing.

10. Once in a while, Mark goes to a national park to be with the trees. He loves walking in the forest.

11. Mark does not want to get married. But he is open to having a like-minded companion.

12. As far as he can, he practices living in the moment with awareness, happiness, and love.

13. Mark's vacations are mostly spent in India. He goes to his favorite retreat for three weeks every year. Seeing new places is not his way of traveling.

INTEGRITY

The present moment is the best present.
The grass is the greenest right under the nose.

The qualities of a Sattwic person:

1. A person with fully blossomed integrity clearly knows that the present moment must be lived in fulfillment and nothing else is real. Worries of the future or regrets about the past do not disturb his mind.

2. As his mind is peaceful with regard to the imagination and turmoil about past and future, he can easily come to right conclusions and clear decisions. He is never fickle-minded as he understands that it serves no purpose to dilly-dally.

3. While solving a problem, he may take his time in thinking about the various possibilities, but once he is clear and has taken a stand, he sticks to his guns, whatever the general opinion is.

4. His means are his ends. Doing things with awareness, love, and happiness is what he likes. His undertakings are full of some compassionate purpose.

5. He never wavers from his dharma and from the path of righteousness.

6. His priorities are clear and he lives accordingly. He understands the difference between "urgent" and "important."

7. In his meditation, he easily attains stillness and bliss. In his interactions, he practices loving kindness.

8. His needs are limited and he hardly has any desires or ambitions. His sense organs are satisfied and he does not care what others think about him.

9. Between peace and excitement, he always goes for peace. Normally, he does not prefer a hectic lifestyle, but for a right cause, he does not mind getting into activity also.

10. He does not appreciate the imaginary boundaries of nationality, language, religion, sex, family, wealth, etc. For him, whosoever is in front of him is worthy of respect and love. Even plants and animals receive unconditioned love from him.

11. His life is happily disciplined. He has a clear spiritual goal and a path to achieve it. He does not need variety even in spirituality.

THE LADDER OF EVOLUTION

Dissatisfaction has a beautiful silver lining —
It helps you grow.

1. In order to understand the essential needs of
a human mind, let us now study the ladder of
evolution. This will give you an idea about how
the mind evolves. The criteria of evolution are
peace and loving kindness — and realization of
the absolute Truth is the ultimate possibility.

There are seven rungs on the ladder of human evolution:

2. At the lowest rung, you see turmoil and confusion. It is a *lethargic mind*, whose qualities have
been enumerated in detail earlier. Disorder,
chaos, running in circles, indecisiveness,
procrastination, aimless living, baseless fears
and worries, blaming, criticizing, jealousy, guilt,
hatred, unquenchable remorse, mood swings,
and, in extreme cases, viciousness, are the traits
of lethargy. One resorts to alcohol, drugs, television, and useless gossiping, etc., to run away
from the inner noise, but nothing gives satisfaction for more than a few hours. While using

these X factors, there is the facility of ease, i.e., one does not need to make any effort. But the fulfillment coming from them is as transient as a bubble.

3. *When dissatisfaction takes place with one's current state of being, one moves up on the ladder of evolution.* If one is satisfied with the current ways of thinking and living, there is no reason that one will like to move from there. *It is also not necessary that the movement must take place in everybody's life.* In most cases, one lifetime is too short a time to outgrow the current rung.

4. The next rung is the *sensual state.* The X factory of sensuality consists of sensual pleasures, status, attachment with people, ambitions, and endless activity. This has also been discussed before. A sensual person has many desires and expectations and he always lives in hopes and fears related to the future. While fulfilling his desires, he does get the experience of pleasure and excitement, but the price he pays for it is enormous. He is never peaceful and happy. His life is a continuous struggle for attaining, achieving, and accumulating. He lives in a state of stress most of the time.

5. A few get fed up with this lifestyle and decide to take the next step, which is toward the *aesthetic-creative* state of consciousness. Now, some subtlety starts developing in the mind. One's attention and love turn toward the *intelligence type(s)* one is strong in. It means one revels in one's natural dharma grooves.

6. These are the six intelligence types or dharmas created by nature:

   a. Linguistic: Love for fiction, nonfiction, philosophy, oratory, poetry, etc.

   b. Mathematical-logical: Love for the natural sciences, mathematics, modern philosophy, statistics, etc.

   c. Musical: Love for music — vocal and/ or instrumental.

   d. Kinesthetic: Love for sports, yoga, swimming, athletics, etc.

   e. Spatial: Love for colors and space as experienced by architects, designers, sculptors, etc.

   f. Intrapersonal: Love for psychology, psychotherapy, and related fields.

7. The aesthetic-creative state is the first step in bringing about some Sattwa in the mind. Now one's concentration and stability grow. Even the duration and quality of happiness

become better. Somebody in this state will love studying books, going to operas and classic movies, spending evenings in swimming pools or on football grounds, dancing, listening to or making music, painting, or similar pursuits. One experiences a lot of joy in following one's favorite activity.

8. However, when one is not doing what one likes doing, one is either bored or just drags on. The creativity has a shadow aspect of pride also: the I-know-the-best attitude. Many creatives live unhappy lives as they are emotionally very sensitive and don't know how to let go of the negative feelings. Moreover, the direction of creativity is externalized and one hardly has any understanding about one's own mind. The application of creativity for uplifting one's consciousness is a different game altogether.

9. The next milestone is the state of *compassion* in which one understands that without opening the heart, something will always remain missing. Here, the attachment with an intelligence type gets sublimated into attachment with a cause. For example, it is not just physics that remains a motivating factor; it will also be love of humanity for which physics will be studied. It is not just

the love for music, but also its soothing and enlivening effects on the listeners that becomes a driving force. Selfless love becomes important now and one consciously takes steps to develop it.

10. There is no doubt that it is beautiful to have a compassionate heart, but it has its own limitations:

    a. A compassionate person is passionate about a cause; but if he does not achieve the desired results, he gets put off. He is still too dependent on success and failure. He might not be doing things for any selfish ends, but even this selflessness can become a cause of pain, if it is not based upon correct understanding of the three qualities of the mind. He wants to bring about *quick* and *lasting* changes in the society, but he does not understand that most people take their own sweet time to change.

    b. He gets burnt out with time. In our meditation retreats, most of our students belong to this state of consciousness. What beautiful hearts they have! Many of them come to India just to do some volunteer work, just to give some comfort to the suffering humanity. Yet we have seldom met anybody who is peaceful just because he is compassionate. Lasting peace requires something more.

c. Too much sensitivity also affects him in his interactions with others. He may easily get disturbed by what others think about him or his passion. He also does not know the art of balancing his feelings with his understanding.

11. There comes a time in the life of a compassionate person when he starts searching for some more enriching avenues. The next step is the state of *introspection* in which the mind turns inward and starts asking questions about the nature of the Self, the causes of unhappiness, the way to peace, etc. One starts inquiring as to what is real and unreal; what is the source of all that appears to the senses — the whence and whither of the universe. This inquiry takes one to the most important question that one can ever ask oneself: "*Who am I?*" Actually, it is a long journey before one deserves asking this supreme question, but when the ripe time comes, one starts doing this deepest reflection on one's own true Self.

12. The process of evolution within the state of introspection can be slightly different for each person. But mostly, one grows through these steps:

   a. Studying self-help books to learn how to become strong in mind and how to have better concentration.

   b. Turning toward spiritual texts or places or teachers to understand more about the inner-growth possibilities.

   c. Practicing meditation, which is more of a concentration practice in the beginning.

   d. As one grows further, one may start following any of the three main paths of meditation: the path of knowledge, devotion, or awareness. All of them lead to the same goal. Which path one will follow depends upon one's own natural inclination.

   e. In the initial stages, there is hardly any integration of the study with one's real life. There is dichotomy in theory and practice and one is still lost in the illusions of duality, reality, permanence, and incompleteness. One has a vague understanding about the true purpose of meditation, but one is not able to live up to it.

f. Slowly, one recognizes that it is not possible to quiet the mind in meditation unless these concepts are lived in one's day-to-day life. It means one makes the following efforts and eventually realizes their fruition:

- Experiencing fulfillment within oneself — independent of X factors and conditionings.
- Living in awareness, peace, and love each moment.
- Helping others without expectations.
- Faith in the teachings.
- Happy acceptance of people as they are.
- Using difficulties of life as growth opportunities.
- Considering fulfillment more important than excitement.
- Considering purity more important than lust.
- Considering peace more important than anger and irritation.
- Considering detachment more important than attachment.
- Considering contentment more important than greed.
- Considering humility more important than pride.

- Noninterference in the business of others.
- Not judging, blaming, or criticizing others.
- Loving oneself in peace and in one's own dharma.

g. As one progresses further in meditation, one realizes that the *notion of possession is also a dream.* "That this house or money or person is mine" is the cause of so much suffering in this world. The sense of possession leads to desires, fears, and insecurities. They, in turn, cause the initiation of endless activities. One just keeps running all the time due to these false imaginings!

h. Proceeding further in this inner journey of meditation, *the idea that "I am this body-mind complex" is also shaken up.* As one detaches from this deepest conditioning of the mind, one realizes that one's true nature is divine. One experiences one's identity with the Self — the light of eternal blissful awareness. Initially, the experience comes only for a short duration, but with practice, its duration becomes much more stable. This experience matures with practice. At first, there is an oscillatory movement between remembrance and forgetting. With sincere meditation, one gets established in the Self as one's true reality.

13. Until the experience of one's identity with the eternal blissful awareness becomes stable, it is called the *state of introspection.* When vacillation and forgetfulness cease completely and there is continuity in the experience of the Self, it is called the *state of Self establishment.* Now, it is no longer a far-off concept. It is one's true identity. One realizes that one's true nature is self-luminous and eternal — there was never a time when one was not and there will never be a time when one will be not. Coming into being and ceasing to be does not happen in the reality of the Self — these are just notions of the mind.

14. This remarkable realization brings about a complete change in the perception of reality. The world, with all its concepts, conditionings, and relationships, becomes a nonentity. It is seen to be a long dream, rooted only in wrong notions.

15. After Self establishment, there is only one last step left on the ladder of evolution — the enlightenment, the experience of final liberation from this mortal world. Here, the

small wave merges back into the infinite ocean! The notion that "I am a separate Self" is given up when the experience of union with the Cosmic Self takes place. One realizes that there is only one reality that has superimposed upon itself infinite names, forms, and qualities. *It means that the three-fold differentiation between the knower, the known, and the knowledge gets annihilated. Only One remains. It is the experience of the Universal Consciousness, Blissful and Eternally Aware. "I am the Self" gets sublimated into "I am not; only That is." Total and unequivocal surrender takes place and one always lives in nonforgetfulness of this absolute Truth.*

16. This is the ladder of evolution. You will see that on the lowest rung — lethargy — there is total chaos and confusion. On the highest rung, there is the purest awareness and bliss. In between, there are steps for growing. One very important fact is that *it is not possible to skip the steps.* It is just not possible for a lethargic or sensual mind to straightaway jump to the state of liberation. One has to pass through and outgrow the rungs on the way. What is possible, however, is that one can expedite the process by

bringing conscious intensity, sincerity, and perseverance into one's practice.

17. If you introspect over your own life, it is possible that you will find yourself oscillating between lethargy and introspection. You may love reflecting over spiritual truths, but you may also have your lethargic/sensual tendencies. In the initial phase of spirituality, you don't want to detach from your previous habit patterns. It shows that you have a good potential for spiritual life, but you are yet not serious enough for your growth. You are still wavering. In order to come out of this state, you need to spend most of your time in your higher states of being. You should try to meditate more deeply and study the scriptures that teach you the essence of spirituality. Such books can easily be found in all religions.

18. There are two ways in which one's evolution can take place:

   a. **Natural evolution**: You go through the experiences of various pairs of opposites — success-failure, gain-loss, praise-blame, etc. — and slowly learn from them. The so-called bad experiences give you detachment and the so-called good experiences lead to attachment. You oscillate between them and learn your lessons slowly. It takes you a long time to understand that happiness resides within you.

b. **Revolutionary evolution**: You contemplate, meditate, and thereby outgrow illusions and desires. It involves clear understanding, deep honesty, and indomitable courage.

19. There is an ancient story of two birds, Sam and Peter. They used to live on two different branches of a tree. Sam was living on the lowest branch and Peter was on the highest. Sam was ever dissatisfied with life. He used to be discontented with the quality of fruits that came on the tree — the fruits of the other trees appeared to be better. He always felt that others were living happier lives. And Peter — he was ever serene and fulfilled; always indrawn and full of gratitude.

Sam's life was full of happenings. If he ate a bitter fruit, he would feel bad and would look up to Peter who was always happy. He would think in those moments of distress how peaceful and contented Peter was. There always arose a desire to be like Peter and then he would jump up to the next higher branch. On that branch, he would

look for fruits again. On eating a sweet
fruit, he would ask for more and more
sweet fruits. But on eating bitter fruits, the
suffering made Sam move up to the next
higher branch. Slowly and slowly, after many
years of eating sweet and bitter fruits, Sam
reached the highest branch of the tree and
a miracle happened there... Sam merged
into Peter! He realized that he was ever one
with his friend. The distance was just an
imagination. They were actually always one.

20. Yes, the distance is imaginary. Your highest
possibility is a state of your mind. You are
only postponing its realization by holding
on to various illusions. You are one with
Buddha, Christ, and Krishna. Just accept
it and start living. If you cannot, you may
have to consume many bitter fruits in life.
The choice is yours. If you want to go
through the tedious and long process of
natural evolution because your desires are
too strong, it is perfectly fine; but you must
keep in mind the consequences. You should
not blame anybody else, later on. If you
think that you can get true happiness from
the external world of senses, just try; and
keep trying. There is going to come a day

in your life when you yourself will shun this illusion as poison.

21. Normally, much change does not occur in the life of an unconscious person. Unless one is *sincerely working* to outgrow one's given character-patterns, one just dies with the same mindset that one was born with.

22. However, *if you want to hit the target without delay, meditation is the only way.* Sincere and systematic practice of right understanding is the master key to opening the gate of true freedom.

WHY IS IT DIFFICULT TO MEDITATE?

Lethargics and sensuals cannot understand meditation.
For others, success depends upon honesty.

Let me tell you about two people whom I've known for many years. Vijayashree is a funny character. She tells everybody that she is very happy, but wants to poke her nose in everybody's affairs! She thinks that God has been gracious to her, but also has endless desires! She believes that she accepts people with love, but gets disturbed at the drop of a hat! She feels that she does not care what others are thinking about her, but wants to talk about herself even with strangers! When you try to tell her that she is hooked to so many things and if she wants to be happy, she has to unhook herself, she immediately becomes defensive and tells you that she is already unhooked and detached from everything!

Shambhavi is also a normal human being. She did a Z Meditation retreat in 2005. At that time, she appeared a bit disturbed. She told me that she had no desires left except one — she wanted to live in a big house with an area of about ten thousand square feet! She was then living in an apartment, which was not suitable to her high standards! During the retreat, she said that she was very peaceful and did not have even one disturbing thought to do the work on! However, we noticed that she was overcareful about her appearance and makeup.

*If anyone would say anything negative about how she looked, she
would get defensive and brood over it for a long time.*

*A few years later, her "only" desire got fulfilled. Her husband
bought her a big house in the locality where she wanted to live.
But things had changed by then. She did not want that house
anymore! The reason for coming to the retreat again was that her
relationship with her husband was acrimonious and she wanted
to get a divorce! She had only this desire left — this time!*

1. Both Vijayashree and Shambhavi have a
   wide gap between what they think about
   themselves and their true reality. Both of
   them have countless disturbing thoughts
   — as their basic character is sensual. Their
   minds are so restless that they cannot
   understand and accept their reality. It is not
   that they are lying. They just cannot gauge
   their real state.

2. When one is attached to the three qualities, it is extremely difficult to do any work
   on the mind. Most of the people in our
   world are like that. For them, the illusion of
   incompleteness is not an illusion. They truly
   feel that they would get their happiness
   through the desire-fulfillment route. Hence,
   it is difficult — almost impossible — for
   them to internalize the gaze and meditate.

TRUE MEANING OF PRACTICE

Without leisure, it is difficult to meditate.

Swami Chinmay was sitting cross-legged on his pillow at his bed. He was using the back of his bed for support as he was feeling very weak. He was almost one hundred years of age and he was getting an intuition that on the coming full moon day, he would leave his body and merge into the absolute.

His mind was as clear as the sky. His eyes were closed and there was a smile on his face. For the last eighty years, he had lived the life of a monk and in the last twenty years, he had been acting as the Head of Atmananda Monastery. He had several bright disciples — some monks and some householders.

Throughout his life, he had fulfilled all duties as a service to the Lord. Now, in his last days, he was spending most of his time meditating and teaching his disciples. But there was one responsibility still left to be finished. He had to select his successor. He was thinking about each of his disciples and two names were foremost in his mind: Ananda and Yoga. These were two disciples who had never refused any command of his. He knew that both of them could give their lives, if he ever asked them. They also used to love each other like real brothers.

Swami Chinmay knew that Yoga was selflessness personified. Everybody in the monastery loved him. He was always busy looking after the welfare of the inhabitants. Anybody could go to his room at all times. It had often happened that they would wake him up at night just for some very simple problems. He would never mind people taking him for granted. He felt that doing selfless service to those who lived at the monastery was the service to the Lord as well as to his teacher, Swami Chinmay.

However, Swami felt that Yoga was not giving enough time to his meditation. He could work twenty-four hours a day. But he could not sit still even for one hour. On the other hand, Ananda was the embodiment of blissful awareness. He would spend most of his time studying the scriptures and doing meditation. When he was not sitting in meditation, he would not let any thought go by unnoticed. He would be aware of the mind all the time. Even before going to sleep, he would keep watching his thoughts and doing his mantras. His sole goal in life was Self Realization. He was totally dedicated to attaining this goal. But this did not mean that he would not do his duties happily. He would also be there to help any of his brothers, but it was not in his nature to go out of his way and create new activities. All monks of the monastery respected him in the same way they respected the Swami.

It did not take Swami much time to come to a decision. He chose Ananda as his successor because he knew that although Yoga had a gem of a heart, he was still very restless. He didn't have any material desires in his mind, but the "force of activity in the mind" was not letting him work on his thoughts. He was too busy, too busy to be able to internalize his gaze and attain his real Self. Swami knew that unless one detached from endless activities, it was not possible to be truly aware.

Swami Chinmay decided in favor of Ananda as his goal of Self Realization was clear and he was completely devoted to attaining it. Nothing else was important for him. There was not even an iota of doubt in his mind that the world was just an illusory dream and the Self was the only reality.

A congregation of five thousand monks was called and when Swami Chinmay announced his decision, it was Yoga who stood up first and bowed to his brother Ananda. Seeing this, Swami Chinmay closed his eyes, thanked God for everything, and breathed his last.

1. Not only will those who have endless desires find it difficult to meditate, but also people who are overactive will discover meditation to be tough. Many seekers keep themselves too occupied as they feel that they are doing God's work or this busy-ness itself is their practice. But in most such cases, the minds remain ever turbulent as not much attention is paid to what is happening inside of oneself. Without leisure, it is difficult to meditate.

LAWS OF PEACE

Respect nature and it will love you.

1. Imagine somebody jumping from the fiftieth story of a building because he believes that he can flout gravity!

2. Imagine somebody putting her bare hands in fire because she believes that she can defy fire!

3. Imagine somebody running his car without gas, as he believes that he can resist friction!

4. You can very well imagine what will happen in all these cases. It is not possible to challenge the laws of nature. You can invent things like airplanes and fireproof gloves, but they also follow certain other laws of nature. Nature is supreme. You have to use it intelligently. If you abuse it in any way, you will have to pay the price.

5. The same is true for the internal nature of humans. If you want to be peaceful, you need to follow certain laws. *Happiness and peace of mind are governed by these laws.* If you follow them

wisely, you will live peacefully. If you abuse them, suffering will result.

6. It means that *happiness and peace need to be learned.* You may not be born with them. You are brought up with many condition-ings that generally go against these eternal peace principles. You need to learn and apply these principles in order to annul the damaging effects of these societal and congenital beliefs.

7. Spirituality is an objective science. If you follow its laws, you will live in happiness. If you don't, you will live in suffering and restlessness.

Let us now study the seven laws of peace.

FIRST LAW OF PEACE

What is, is.

Adi was doing her third meditation retreat with us. This time, she was struggling with the thought, "Why did my boyfriend leave me?" It was very hard for her to accept that a relationship of nine years could end the way it did. She felt that it was not due to any fault of hers. Eyal, her boyfriend, told her he had suddenly grown attracted to somebody else and was no longer in love with her. She was also wondering if it really was a sudden happening.

1. What were Adi's possible choices?

   a. Eyal living with his new girlfriend + Adi upset and grieving.

   b. Eyal realizing his mistake, apologizing, coming back + happy life ever after!

   c. Adi accepting the change in Eyal + Eyal gone from her life.

2. Adi and Eyal had already discussed it at length and then decided to split up. So the second possibility was not possible at all. That means Adi was left with only two choices: the first and the third. Eyal was already gone. In the first scenario, there was suffering and in the third,

there was peace. What would any sane person do if she does not want to suffer?

3. She might say that life is not mathematics. I understand that, but I will still ask her again: "What choices do you have?"

4. Nature is playing her marvelous game in which coming into being, growth, decay, and death are inevitable occurrences. It happens with everything that has name and form. It happens with relationships also. If you accept it, you live in peace. If you resist, you live in pain. But your living in pain does not stop nature from following her ways.

5. Nature has strewn such beautiful qualities all around us. These five elements, these sense organs, these sense objects, these minds with lethargy, sensuality, and integrity, these mountains, these rivers, these big egos, these compassionate hearts, these greedy minds, these pleasures, these pains... the list is endless. Everything here is a marvel. If you are not seeing, you must be blind — blinded by your ego, your desires, your attachments, and your dependence. When the mind is restless, it cannot enjoy the reality as it is too attached, and too wavering, and too confused. When it is

detached, it can attain awareness and acceptance of life's happenings. Then betrayal
is not frowned upon. It is rather looked
at with noninterference, compassion,
and peace.

6. What is, is. What was, was. What will be,
will be. "I wish it were different" means
suffering. Expectations mean chaos. *If it is
not mathematics, it is painful.*

7. So many students of Z Meditation have
told me that these three simple words have
brought about the biggest change in their
lives! They say they learned to live happily
only after learning this simple law of peace:
What is, is!

Second Law of Peace

Acceptance is peace.

1. Adi's third choice is the only one that will give her peace. Her options are simple: acceptance or nonacceptance. If she accepts that it is possible that people can change and it can happen in her life also, she will be peaceful. If she doesn't, it will be very, very painful.

2. "Relationship" is a notion and its various definitions vis a vis different people in our life are nice but mostly wrong. These definitions are nothing but our dependence and expectations garbed in nice words. One such idea that most of us believe in is "Breakups should never happen." When the reality does not match this idea, affliction takes place. The reality is that breakups do happen. If Eyal is leaving Adi, it is just an inevitable event in the cosmos. Nonacceptance of the inevitable is what leads to pain.

3. If you want to have peace of mind, you will need to accept all of the following in your life — without any ifs, or buts:

a. *Three qualities of mind* — People are the way they are. They are obsessively following their own character-patterns that are rooted in the three qualities — Tamas, Rajas, and Sattwa. They cannot help thinking and doing what they think and do. They are helplessly driven by their minds.

b. *Past and future* — Past exists only in one's transient mental formations — one's memory. Future cannot be known or controlled by anybody. Unconscious dwelling in them always spoils the present by causing restlessness and worries. We cannot even control the results of our actions. The only thing we can control is how we are acting and reacting in this present moment. We *can* choose to live in awareness, love, and happiness — that is very much within our domain.

c. *The present circumstances* — This present moment is our opportunity to grow in detachment, fulfillment, understanding, and love. Why miss it? If it is a difficult situation, we need to make full use of it for learning detachment, strengthening our endurance, and growing spiritually. Peace needs to be learned. One may not be born with it, but one can certainly study and practice for growing in it.

d. *The inevitable* — One spiritual master was asked by his students why he never felt unhappy. He answered, "Unhappiness is the direct result of nonacceptance of change. One who can accept change will never be unhappy." People will change; the amount of money we have will change; status will change, everybody will get old; beauty will never remain. One who is ever ready and alert about acceptance can never be unhappy. Rather, he will be aware and peaceful.

e. *The necessary* — What ought to be done, what is obligatory in the given circumstances, and what is the righteous course of action have to be freed from the clutches of dilemmas. Things might be unpleasant, but if they are right then there ought to be no vacillation in execution.

4. When we accept the above five, our life will naturally get filled with peace and joy. But if there is resistance, pain will surely follow.

THIRD LAW OF PEACE

Resistance is pain.

1. Adi was initially resisting the reality, but she was
    sincerely looking for a way to come out of her
    pain. In the end, as her resistance waned, she
    experienced peace and freedom. She realized
    that she was actually not attached to Eyal. She
    was attached to a state of fulfillment, which she
    thought would come from him. As she dropped
    this illusion, she regained the awareness that
    she was already fulfilled. She was mistakenly
    identifying it with Eyal.

2. Resistance to the reality is resistance to nature.
    We are supposed to understand that an apple
    will never taste like a mango and an eggplant
    will never taste like beans. They are different.
    They are just different. Without interfering
    in the nature of an apple, we have to learn to
    enjoy it as it is. Lethargy always has the bitter
    smell of confusion and chaos; sensuality must
    result in greed, attachment, and pain; friends
    may not be considerate all the time; love may
    not get reciprocated always. Accepting all

possibilities will lead to peace. Resistance to the inevitable will always be painful.

3. A question is often asked in the meditation retreat: "What about injustice? Should we accept that too and do nothing against it?" Once a student asked, "Why did Gandhi fight injustice being perpetrated by the British? Why didn't he accept it peacefully?"

Here, we need to see whether the actions are happening for a state of completeness or from a state of completeness. Everybody around Gandhi was living in a mindset that unless the British left the country, they could not be happy. But for Gandhi, who was living from a state of completeness, the means were the ends. Following his dharma — righteous politics — with equanimity, love, and peace was an end in itself.

The important point here is that while you fight injustice, your mind should remain as peaceful and balanced as the Himalayas. Without getting perturbed from within, you have to practice the art of equanimity.

4. Let us contemplate on this saying: *The destination is living in freedom and it can be done only in the NOW.*

The Beauty Called "Problems of Life"

Problems are good.

There was a devotee of God whose only desire in life was to meet God. He loved God more than anybody else — even more than himself.

One day God decided to pay him a visit. Early in the morning, there was a knock at the devotee's door. He opened the door and saw God standing in front. His eyes were filled with tears of joy. He started dancing and singing hymns in praise of God. God kept His eyes closed and listened to him with rapt attention. He was spellbound seeing his devotion and love.

After some time, God had to leave and before leaving, God requested him to ask for a boon. The devotee said that his only desire — to meet God — was already fulfilled. He did not want anything. But if God really wanted to give him something, he just desired that he should not have any more desires and he should always follow God's commands. God said, "I am very pleased with you. Your desire will be fulfilled."

As God came out of his house, the devotee caught hold of His hand and asked Him to give the first command. God showed him a big rock in front of his house and asked him to push it. Then God disappeared and the devotee went to the rock and started pushing it. Not only for that day, he started pushing the rock every day — from morning till evening. This became his daily worship of God — following His command to the letter and spirit.

This went on for a few months and he was feeling eternally blissful. However, the villagers did not understand him at all. They were very doubtful about his vision of God and asked him to prove it. They further asked him why that rock was not moving at all even after months of pushing. The devotee prayed to God to help him. Every day he would pray to God to come for help. But God didn't come. One day, out of total disgust, he decided that he would not push the rock anymore.

That night, God appeared to him in a dream and asked him why he gave up pushing the rock. He said that it was not moving and he did not understand the benefit of the whole exercise. He then asked God to explain the benefit.

God said, "What do you mean by 'benefit'? Don't you see that your muscles — both physical and mental — are becoming stronger with each passing day? You are growing in endurance, fortitude, perseverance, and patience. You are learning to face the ridicules of people. Is it a small benefit for you? What more do you want?"

    1. Push Your Rocks: The same rock attitude applies to our life as well. The rocks of life are the problems we face, every day. Pushing these rocks, we become stronger in equanimity, peace, endurance, fortitude, and understanding. The problematic situations or rocks will always be there. There will always be difficult people on the way. Their only job would be to cross our lines of progress. There will always be sickness and hospitalization of oneself or of some dear ones. There will always be some birth somewhere and death elsewhere. How can anybody avoid failures and keep winning all the time? How can you make everybody very considerate and remove all negativities from their behavior? These are the inevitables of life. You accept them, good for you. You resist them, bad for you as they will still be there and you will be disturbed too.

2. When your priorities are pointing outward, you get bogged down by difficulties. You don't want them in your life. You just want to reach your goals quickly. There is haste, impatience, and unawareness in your behavior. Nature gives difficulties so that your inner obstacles surface and you become aware of them. How else will you understand them and make an effort to remove them?

3. When the priorities get internalized, i.e., your inner growth becomes paramount for you, your attitude changes completely

toward the problems. You *try* to solve them one by one — and to the best of your capabilities. That's it. They get solved, good. They don't get solved, that's also fine. You accept that you cannot find the solutions to all problems. Nobody can do that. Problems are opportunities of growth for you. You know that you can only do your best with love, awareness, and happiness. The rest — only God knows!

4. You also need to understand that all solutions are the seeds of new problems. Something or other will always be there in life. Always! You are only expected to do things with peace, love, and awareness — day after day.

FOURTH LAW OF PEACE

Completeness = Lack of incompleteness

1. Once a Zen master was asked: "What is the essence of your teachings?" He said, "You don't have to do anything. You don't need to go anywhere. You are not required to become anybody."

2. "Life" is filled with happiness up to the brim. The true nature of everybody is bliss eternal. Don't take it as a cliché, please. You can yourself experience this bliss — you just need to follow certain principles. It is like trying to see distant stars with naked eyes. You can't do it because the scope of the eyes is limited. You need to use certain other laws of nature to act as a bridge between your eyes and the stars. A telescope is not a physical instrument. It is the essence of a few laws of nature. It is intelligence in physical form.

3. True happiness also needs a bridge. In fact, it is a very near star that appears to be distant. There are certain laws of internal nature that act as a bridge that can take you to the experience of

lasting happiness. The essence of those laws is "*You don't need to desire and chase. Your true nature is happiness itself.*" It is this desiring only that is acting as a hindrance. Just drop it. Can happiness be experienced if you feel incomplete inside of you?

4. *True completeness has only one definition: **Lack of incompleteness.*** I = C. The moment you accept I + X = Completeness as a way of your life, you have already admitted defeat. You are indirectly supporting incompleteness. You are imposing certain absurd conditions in order to realize in a distant future what is currently available to you. Your postponement is not only unnecessary, it is also futile.

5. Imagine a state in which you no longer believe that X factors are imperative for you. How would you feel? If you feel bad, you are still clinging. If you feel light and good, you have understood it right. Having understood this mechanism of the mind, you need to practice living in this state of freedom.

6. Besides money and status, the most important X factor that influences your mind is your dependence on people who affect you

in three ways. It is called *ICA syndrome* —
infatuation, controlling others, and seeking
approval from others. If you have any of the
three, life can never be easy.

I. Who does not know that dependence
upon somebody else causes pain in the
long run? Why does it happen that in the
West, 50% of marriages meet their end in
legal separation?

C. Ask yourself: "Do I feel happy when I
want others to follow me and they choose to
follow their own heart? Or, when they follow
me with an unwilling heart?"

A. When I seek approval and appreciation,
how do I feel? Am I grounded in awareness
and happiness?

FIFTH LAW OF PEACE

Pain is what you get when you step out of your own business and start interfering in others' business.

1. The most stressed people in the world are those who are in the habit of interfering in other people's business. They are always curious about others. They have a false sense of superiority. They think they know the best. In reality, they know the least — even about themselves.

2. There are three kinds of businesses in this world: my business, your business, and nature's business. When one is in the habit of minding just one's own business, one grows. When one pokes one's nose everywhere, one suffers. The beauty of this game is that one does not understand that one is suffering. Anger, resentment, restlessness, pride, stress, worries, and jealousy, etc., are not taken as suffering! These are understood to be life's inherent necessities and essential experiences!

3. Those who criticize others are *always* found wanting in the same areas that they criticize about. Living in glass houses, they like throwing

stones at others! When others do the same, they don't like it!

4. We also need to understand the difference between thoughtful compassion and impulsive interference. For example, as regards your duty toward your children, your dharma is to provide them with the right environment and the best possibilities of growth. But even after having done your best, they may not follow what you think is the best course for them. You will have to draw a line somewhere, lest your own mind should get disturbed.

5. *Do your best and leave the rest.* While helping others, the possibility that you may not get the desired response or your compassion may get misunderstood is always there. Always be prepared for these eventualities.

6. How would you recognize the difference between interference and compassion? The former creates disturbance in your mind and the latter gives you the experience of pure joy. In the second case, you just do your best without imposing any outcome.

Sixth Law of Peace

You cannot change the past.
You cannot control the future.

Ayala and her family had a strong bond of love with their relations in Israel. They were always there for each other in difficult times.

In 1999, they migrated to Canada as they got a great business opportunity. Unfortunately, Ayala's sister passed away within one year of their leaving Israel. When Ayala came to Z Meditation Retreat, we realized that she was severely suffering from a strong sense of remorse that it was because of their going to Canada that her sister went into a depression and died. She felt that if she had not gone away, her sister would have lived longer.

1. Many of us are in the habit of unnecessarily finding fault with ourselves. Then we start lamenting, regretting, or feeling guilty for something we haven't done. This happens because of a lack of clear thinking and nonacceptance of reality.

2. If your intentions are not to harm anybody and something happens just by providence, you are absolutely not responsible. Just pray, bless, and help. You should not take it to heart. Having

clarity in thinking and loving yourself are your foremost responsibilities.

3. However, if something untoward happens through intent and later on you continue feeling bad about it for a long time, this is also not helpful. *Regret, remorse, and guilt are useful only when you resolve to do it differently the next time.* It is human to make mistakes. It is normal and natural. Life does not end there. We need to learn our lessons, let go of the past, and move forward.

4. Can we ever undo the past? The past exists only in wavy mental formations — just some memories. The actual happening is already over and it can never be changed. We spoil our perfect present by clinging to the futile wish that the past should have been different. Nobody can change the past. The idea itself is so hopeless and absurd!

5. The same with the future too — it exists as mental formations only. These formations create another trap of unhappiness! Nobody can control what is going to happen three minutes from now. Nobody! You can only live up to your best potential in the present. And that is your sole obligation.

6. When there are worries and insecurities about the future, are you more efficient in handling the job at hand? What will be more favorable for a good future — a restless mind or a restful mind? What is more helpful in finding solutions to your problems — turbulence or peace?

7. One day, you are going to give up all that you are attached to. Just think if it is really worth it — trying to change the past or control the future. When you live in the past or the future, you lose the joy of the moment. Is it *prudent* to do so?

SEVENTH LAW OF PEACE

What they say about me has nothing to do with who I am.
Who knows me better than myself?

David came home one day and his wife, Julia, started whining, as usual. She had seen David and Margaret together in a restaurant and she jumped to various conclusions: "You are in a relationship with Margaret. You have been lying to me. You don't care for me. I already sensed it a few months before... blah... blah... blah."

It was true that David had gone to lunch with Margaret. They were very good friends and that was it.

Poor David! He got defensive and tried to pacify his wife. But the more he tried to explain, the worse it became. Julia was not listening at all. In a few days her mental phantoms became so huge and uncontrollable that she decided to leave him for good.

1. When we met David in Dharamsala, he was a devastated man. He believed that his divorce happened because of his inept handling of the situation! He felt that if he had not gone to lunch with Margaret, Julia would not have left him. It was all his fault.

2. What do you think was the best course of action for David? Was he responsible for Julia's

suspicion? Was he at fault anywhere in the whole episode? Was he right in feeling guilt and remorse that Julia left him due to a stupid mistake on his part? Should he not have gone to the restaurant with Margaret? Who knows the truth better — David or Julia?

3. It is such an absurdity that you judge yourself using the understanding of others, even when you know that they are wrong! Are you responsible for what goes on in the minds of others? Can't you find for yourself who you truly are and what your intentions were in a particular situation? If others are not in a mood to listen to your truth, is it your responsibility?

4. This is an important spiritual practice for all of us – **not to take anything personally**. There will be opinion cyclones and maligning storms blowing all around us. *Take it as a part of your practice. Remain unperturbed. When Sattwa, Rajas, and Tamas function, it is bound to happen.*

5. There is clutter, a noisy clutter in the minds of those who are filled with Tamas and Rajas. Their mess is neither your business nor responsibility. It is not your duty

to silence their noise. You cannot change anybody unless there is a sincere desire to change. If you forcefully try to do so, it will only lead to the feelings of helplessness and pain as most of them will not understand your intentions.

6. There is another aspect here: they might be right in their opinions. Fine. But *who will do the truth check?* Can anybody else do it for you? If somebody tells you that you are a liar, just do the truth check. Do you lie? If yes, feel grateful to the person that he has helped you become aware. If no, tell him with all your compassion that he is wrong. You don't need to fight. You don't need to be defensive. You don't have to give explanations. It is fine that he has a poor opinion about you — it is a rock for you to push in order to grow in detachment and equanimity.

Remember these laws of peace by heart.

When you get up in the morning,

Contemplate on them.

When you go to bed at night,

Contemplate on them.

DEEP INQUIRY

Dig deep.
Dig deeper.

1. Many meditators practice watching their thoughts and try to be indifferent to them. Such mindfulness of restlessness is only a prerequisite for peace. It just gives you a realization that your mind is restless. However, passive mindfulness can only give you relief, but not a cure. Restlessness derives all its food from its roots of desires, incompleteness equations, and conditionings. Now, we will learn how to detach ourselves from these roots.

2. The lasting solution to this universal malady of mental turmoil is *right understanding*. When you change your perspective and drop the illusions, noise will drop on its own. Coming to know that all your suffering was based on wrong notions and absurd ideas, you will love to detach from them. You will feel light and free. When done in the right spirit, it is a very joyful process.

3. Deep Inquiry is a systematic work of digging out the deep-seated roots of agitation. You use a set

of questions to understand why you have been so uneasy in your mind. When you get to know the truth through your *own* rational thinking, the effect is deep as you cannot deny your own findings or challenge what you have yourself discovered.

4. This practice can be a challenge! When you recognize that you were holding on to certain false beliefs that were causing restlessness, you want to give them up. But the next step is tough — really giving them up. You might have cherished them all your life. Not only you, but your parents, your teachers, your psychotherapists, and the entire society also cherish them! Now, you need to flow against the current. You are able to understand what most of them don't and cannot. They may not accept your new way of thinking. They may think that something is wrong with you. It is a challenge to be indifferent and compassionate at the same time.

5. Z Meditation Deep Inquiry is a six-step process of self-questioning that helps you stand aside from your own mind and realize freedom. It happens in this order:

   a. Coming out of the daydreams and understanding their negative utilitarian consequences.

b. Digging out the first roots of *causal feelings* and understanding their consequences in terms of the actual *consequential feelings.*

c. Digging out the second roots of *incompleteness equations* and understanding their implications in terms of impermanence and unfulfillment.

d. Digging out the third roots of *general conditionings* and experiencing happiness and freedom.

e. Understanding the consequences of interfering in others' business and finding out what one's own real business is.

f. Reinforcement questioning for making the effect deep and lasting.

6. In one's practice, one will always need to be vigilant lest the Inquiry will become just a boring routine — like any other meditation practice. To obviate this possibility, you should keep these two checks in mind:

a. Do the Inquiry slowly and mindfully. Don't rush. You don't have to reach anywhere. If you do the questions well, you will be outgrowing your morbid habit patterns. You will then experience a fresh fragrance in your being. What

can be more important than the realization of lasting fulfillment, joy, and love
within oneself?

b. While asking any question, think
   deeply about the consequences of the
   answers that you arrive at. They can be
   life-altering.

INITIAL PREPARATION

Prepare yourself well. The enemy is very strong.

1. There are some initial preparations following which it will become a bit easier for you to meditate:

2. When you sit for meditation, your mind must be fresh. Many times, meditators practice with a tired mind, at the end of the day or after finishing some heavy activity. How is it possible to do that? Some others force themselves to get up early in the morning and do meditation. They experience neither clarity nor upliftment. I am not saying that it should not be done in the morning. It is just that if you are not a morning person, you will not be able to do it with alacrity. *It is better late than lethargic.*

3. Mornings have an advantage, however. You are not hard pressed by your appointments. You can also maintain regularity in your sittings. It can be helpful to start the mornings with some light mindful exercises like yoga or studying a scripture that will help you *wake up*. When the mind becomes alert after a while, you can meditate.

4. If you think mornings are just not possible for you, you may do it in the evening. But you will have to be careful in the evenings, too. Coming back from work or school, you may be too tired to take up the challenge of Deep Inquiry. Also, you may be tempted to go somewhere else, i.e., your priorities might be skewed in the evenings. You will need to be very firm with your resolve.

5. It is always better to have a short nap in the afternoon or in the evening so that the mind is refreshed for this important task of facing oneself. Please don't listen to those who are against this idea of napping. They may not require it as they don't meditate. Learn to appreciate that your needs can be different. Have clarity about your requirements and serve them as your important obligations.

6. The stomach should be light when you meditate. On a heavy stomach, the mind tends to become lazy.

7. What you do during the rest of the day has a powerful impact on meditation. You cannot remain irritated with people around and also have a blissful meditation.

8. Meditation is the process of outgrowing your basic character-patterns. It is a serious work for realizing peace, happiness, and compassion in your heart. It cannot be taken as a routine monotonous exercise that you must finish, somehow. You ought to be looking forward to this most beautiful time of the day.

9. An hour a day, at least. Less than that, you will not come to understand the games your mind plays.

10. Be careful. Your friends and company can undo the entire work you do on your meditation seat. Just one comment from somebody can easily bring you back to where you started from. They have so many conditionings alive in their minds. They think that their beliefs are absolutely true. They don't want to change as they apparently derive their happiness from these beliefs. It is not your responsibility to shove the truth in somebody's unwilling throat. But it is indeed your responsibility to remain vigilant so that you can do it for yourself.

11. Systematic and regular practice of one method is a must. You have to be watchful

that you don't indulge in spirituality
hopping. Find your path and walk on it.
All paths are good and can take one to the
same goal. You have to see what suits you
the most.

12. While meditating, the back, neck, and head
    must be in a straight line to ensure alert-
    ness. Shoulders should be relaxed and the
    lower back pulled up. Sitting on a cushion
    and keeping the crossed legs on the ground
    will be helpful for your back. If sitting cross-
    legged is difficult, sit on a stool without
    the back support. Be creative in finding
    the right, comfortable, and stable posture
    for yourself.

THIS MOMENT
MINDFUL MOMENT

When else?

There were four thieves living in the city of Kolkata. One day, they decided to commit burglary in a house on the banks of the river Ganges. They came in a boat when everybody was fast asleep. They tied their boat to a tree and entered the house. It took them two hours to carry off everything precious. Coming out with their loot, they put it in the boat and started rowing it. They were rowing with joy in their hearts as they had become very rich that day. They were discussing what they would do with all that money.

However, things were to happen differently — as dawn came, they were caught by the police right in front of that house!

In their haste, they had forgotten to untie the boat. They were rowing in vain!

1. The same may happen in meditation also. You meet many meditators who are rowing the boat for several years and yet say that they cannot still their minds and find bliss in the practice. They are as restless as they were when they started the practice, years before. You hardly see any change in their behavior also.

2. Why does it happen like that? There are two ways in which you can meditate: you may do it for your growth or you may do it mechanically, unaware of the possibility of change. In the latter case, you do it just because it is fashionable or your teacher has asked you to do it or for any such non-elevating reason. Meditation also becomes one of your daily chores. There is hardly any joy and upliftment in such a practice.

3. Look at the ladder of evolution and you will appreciate the reasons of these divergent behaviors. If the sensual X factory is big or if there is extreme lethargy, the motivation to do meditation will be missing. If one still does it, one must be doing it for some purpose other than outgrowing one's habit patterns.

4. However, if there are not many X factors to hold one back, there is a better possibility that meditation will be deep and joyful.

5. When one becomes aware of the restlessness and suffering and desperately wants to be free, then one initiates the steps to untie the boat. Without disentanglement from one's character-patterns, there is no possibility that it will move freely in the waters

of bliss and awareness. The purpose of *Deep Inquiry is to remove the obstacles in the way of realizing the state of freedom.*

6. In the next few chapters, you are going to learn six questions of Deep Deconditioning Inquiry. These questions need to be applied to the dreams that you get lost in. With the help of Inquiry, you will dig out the roots of restlessness and experience freedom. This is a very unique, creative, beautiful, and efficient way of utilizing one's own thoughts to release the root character-patterns. You will understand that you must face yourself and not try to sweep things under the carpet.

7. Let us learn a simple meditation exercise that will be used as an aid for practicing Inquiry:

Sit straight and bring your awareness to your breath. With the in-breath, you mentally say "This Moment." With the out-breath, you mentally say "Mindful Moment." Be aware of the marvel of breathing. As you are enjoying living in the beauty of the moment, there may arise some disturbing thoughts in your mind. When these involuntary thoughts (or thoughting) are there, your awareness will not be there. However, after some time, naturally, you will get your awareness back. You will realize that you had gotten lost in thoughting. Be aware of the thoughts that disturbed you. In the moments of awareness, these thoughts will vanish. Whatever feelings or other mental formations you were experiencing while dreaming, they will all come to rest. It is just the mindfulness that will remain.

Now, you need to apply to these thoughts the six questions that you will learn. In the initial stage, it is possible that while you are doing this Deep Inquiry, you will again get lost in between. Your involuntary thoughts may knock you out of contemplation. Therefore, it may be helpful doing it in writing. Later on, when you get a firm grasp over the import of the questions, you will be able to do it in your mind as well.

So the method is this: Practice "This Moment. Mindful Moment." with your breathing. When thoughts disturb you, do the full Deep Inquiry and release the attachment with the roots of these thoughts. After that, come back to the practice of "This Moment. Mindful Moment."

In the next chapter, we will learn the first question of Deep Inquiry.

THE FIRST PROFOUND QUESTION

"Is it a dream or reality?"

1. As you become aware of your agitation, stop and ask yourself the first profound question along with its four subquestions:

I. *Is it a dream or reality?*

- Is it relevant in this moment?
- Is it useful in this moment?
- Is it conducive to peace in this moment?
- Am I out of it?

2. The answer to the first question is "dream." Always! If at any point, you find yourself saying that it is a "reality," you haven't understood the question. *You are always asking the question about the mental formations that you were lost in.* The definition of a dream is that it is a mental formation in which one is lost and when one is lost, one takes it to be reality.

3. There are hidden implications in the question "Is it a dream or reality?" These implications include: "How long will I keep living in these dreams? Isn't it high time that I do something

about it? Am I a puppet to my mind? Am
I not suffering due to its restlessness? My
entire life up to now has been spent in
dreaming. Should I not wake up now?"
While we ask the question, we need to
reflect over these connected questions
as well.

4. The first subquestion, "Is it relevant in
    this moment?" means: "Is it important in
    this moment? Even if I feel something
    is important, can I not wait until I finish
    meditation and create the space for clear
    thinking? And if it is really important right
    now, why am I doing meditation and not
    trying to reflect on the problem instead? If
    it is not important in this moment, why am
    I dwelling on it?"

5. The second subquestion, "Is it useful in this
    moment?" means: "Does doing circles in
    one's compulsive imagination lead to any
    solution? Is it useful even from the most
    pragmatic and utilitarian standpoint? Does
    imaginary revolving in the dreams lead to
    any fruits?"

6. The third subquestion, "Is it conducive
    to peace?" means: "Does restlessness
    give peace? Happiness? Do I want to be

peaceful? What is it that I need to do in order to achieve that?"

7. The fourth subquestion, "Am I out of it?" means: "If this question is asked after a night dream, can I ever say *no*? Why? How? What is the inference with respect to my daydreaming? What can be the consequences if I choose to live in awareness and not in dreams? Will they be good and beneficial for me? What is my criterion for goodness?"

8. If my answer to the fourth subquestion is "yes," what is stopping me from always living in awareness?

9. Your world exists in your mind. Your own mind is the *only* direct experience that you always have. You mistakenly identify thoughts with their objects and keep living in this illusion all the time. Detachment from these mental formations is a necessary requirement for realizing peace. If it appears to be difficult, we will go deeper and do some more digging.

10. The next natural question that can come to the mind is, "What then is reality?" There is only one reality — the experience of the moment in which we are in contact with

one marvel of nature or another. We can choose to fill this moment with peaceful enjoyment of these marvels, or we may remain restless in our minds. What is of course not possible is to attain mindfulness and also be restless at the same time.

11. It is an extremely subtle game. It requires all one's sincerity to let go of one's attachment with attachments. If priorities are clear, it can be a very easy task to tame the mind. But if they are not, it can be a great challenge to educate the same mind.

12. Now, as explained in the previous chapter, practice this first profound question with "This Moment. Mindful Moment." exercise for about half an hour and then proceed to the next chapter. As we will go on learning new questions, we will continue to add them to the practice.

Outgrowing Root Character-Patterns

The appearance is just the tip.

1. All of us in this world want to be fulfilled and complete. Nobody wants to remain unfulfilled. Inner completeness is a necessary condition for happiness.

2. Why are people unhappy and restless then? It is due to the imaginary incompleteness and the effort to reach completeness through the route of X factors. If there is incompleteness within, along with the understanding that the fulfillment of certain desires will lead to one's completeness, one will *naturally* have desires, resolves, and restlessness related to that.

3. When one watches one's thoughting while meditating, one realizes that one is mostly undisturbed toward the objects/people/activities one is indifferent to. The thoughts that cause disturbance are always related to one's attachments and desires.

4. When one is lost in the restlessness, one is also lost in its roots. In order to be peacefully happy and complete, one needs to wake up from these roots as well. It means that it is not sufficient to be merely aware of the dreams. That is just the first step. After that, one needs to develop detachment from the deeper levels of dreaming — from one's feelings and incompleteness equations — which form one's deeply ingrained character-patterns. This requires the ability to stand aside and be a witness to one's previous ways of living.

5. Detachment from the root patterns of one's own mind leads to outgrowing them. One can use two prudent perspectives to do that:

   a. *Utilitarian perspective.* What are these patterns useful for? Do they help in getting happiness and fulfillment? Was I prepared for the consequences of restlessness and unhappiness when I accepted these roots as a way of my life?

   b. *Truth perspective.* "Are my beliefs true?" is the most important question for a meditator.

6. *Meditation — blissful residence in eternally pure awareness — cannot be experienced using mechanical means. It requires unwavering adherence to the truth and enduring detachment from false notions.*

THE FIRST ROOT CHARACTER-PATTERN: DESIRES

Desires always create restlessness and suffering.

Carly was a participant in one of the meditation retreats held in 2001. She started traveling in India with her friend Lisa. For the last few days before coming to the retreat, they had been living separately.

What had happened was that one day Lisa called her mother in the U.K. There was a big altercation between them. She got extremely angry and vomited it out on Carly. She came back to the room and started screaming at Carly and insulted her for no apparent reason! She dug out many forgotten stories and called her names.

Carly was naturally disturbed by Lisa's behavior. In the retreat, the scenes of that day kept flashing in her mind. The good times they had spent together, the love that they had for each other, and the way they broke up for no reason — she was having these involuntary dreams all the time.

1. She wanted to be peaceful and learn how to meditate. As she did the first question of the Deep Inquiry, she got some space. She understood that her restlessness was just a mental formation and she was attached to it. While attached, she was lost in it and was considering

it to be something very real. Becoming aware, she realized how useless it was to remain lost. It did not fulfill the related desires and it also did not give her peace.

2. In replying to the fourth subquestion, "Am I out of it?," her first response was "No!" She was not able to detach, despite the understanding that she was trying to detach from a dream only.

3. Why was it difficult for Carly to come out of the daydream? The reason was that she was also attached with the roots of agitation and was completely unaware of it. The first root was her *desire that the breakup should not have happened.* Carly understood that in order to fully come out of dreams, it is necessary to let go of the desires, too. Otherwise, it is not possible at all.

4. Now, she needed to contemplate through the second Deep Inquiry question and understand her feelings. In this process, detachment and letting go happens on its own.

THE SECOND PROFOUND QUESTION

"What are the feelings hidden in the dream?"

1. While answering the fourth subquestion of the first main question, if you say that you are out of the dream and you have clearly understood that detachment from your mental waves constitutes freedom, you have won the first battle. Still, there is a distinct possibility of forgetfulness and getting clouded by your previous patterns again. If, on the other hand, you have not come out of the dream and your understanding is hazy, you need the furtherance of the Deep Inquiry all the more.

2. The second profound question also has four subquestions:

II. *What are the feelings hidden in the dream?*

    a. What are the *causal feelings?* (State all the sets in the form of "I like that..." and "I dislike that...," etc.)

    b. What are the *consequential feelings?*

    c. Do I want to be peaceful?

    d. Keeping the causal feelings alive, can I attain peace?

3. This profound question is meant to help us understand why we get restless. It makes us see if we have happy feelings or unhappy ones. Normally, when you are lost in dreams, there is total involvement in the feelings also. You become one with the feelings. In that situation, it is not possible to understand and work on the mind — one is too lost there.

4. *The causal feelings are: liking and disliking; desire and aversion; love and hate; hope and wish; expectation and craving, etc.* For the sake of simplicity, we will mostly work with *liking and disliking.*

5. There can be more than one set of causal feelings in your mind. Each dream can be loaded with a complex of desires.

6. It is necessary to stand aside and be aware. When you do that, you are out of the feelings. You experience awareness and understanding. You are no longer getting buffeted about by your own mind.

7. The restlessness of your mind is never due to people and things. It is rather due to your desires and expectations that cause all

the suffering and turmoil. When there is indifference, the situations do not cause any flutter in your mind.

8. The consequential feelings are wide-ranging — sadness, anger, depression, dejection, feeling low, burden, boredom, irritation, hatred, frustration, disappointment, weakness, fear, worry, rejection, stress, inferiority, superiority, excitement, pleasure, feeling high, etc.

9. If you want to get rid of your consequential feelings, you have to let go of their causes, too. Keeping your desires and aversions alive, you cannot be peaceful!

10. Now we reach a very important point in the Deep Inquiry — *the right prioritization.* What do you really want in life — the control over the external or the internal? You can of course choose the former, but you will have to be ready to accept the consequences. Desires will always lead to agitation, frustration, anger, and other unhappy feelings. Do you *really* want that?

11. Think deeply. What is it that you are giving up in order to be peaceful? You are not running away to a forest or joining a monastery. You are where you are and you will be

where you will be. It is just that you can now have more room for clarity, if you detach from the causal feelings. You are appreciating and accepting that certain mental formations always give birth to agitation, which you don't want in yourself. You now intelligently decide — without any compulsion — that for you, peace, happiness, and awareness are more important than expecting and hating. You renounce the illusion that desiring will lead to happiness — as it never does.

12. Think more deeply. *What you have decided to detach yourself from is only a dream*; albeit at a deeper subconscious level. Your desires and aversions were also your mental formations. You were just deeply attached and lost in them. You have in reality given up nothing but dreaming!

13. Could Carly be peaceful without dropping her desires? She realized that her consequential feelings of sadness, irritation, and anger were coming from her attachment with the likes-dislikes related to the breakup. She also understood that if she would not let go of this attachment, she could never be peaceful. We will study her Deep Deconditioning Inquiry in the coming chapters.

THE SECOND ROOT
CHARACTER-PATTERN:
INCOMPLETENESS EQUATIONS

Does fulfillment of desires really lead to your fulfillment?

1. Carly cannot attain peace of mind if her desire that Lisa should not have insulted her remains alive. She sometimes feels angry, sometimes sad, and sometimes helpless, and the cause of all this is this desire that it should not have happened.

2. Now, she wants to attain peace at any cost. She does not want to harbor the bitter feelings anymore. She understands that she cannot undo the past. Therefore, she has to give up this desire.

3. In reality, the price of peace is no price at all. It just requires letting go of the imaginary and false connection between desires and happiness. This detachment needs to be earnest and clear. Carly's inquiry went on like this:

I. Is it a dream or reality?

Dream. Only my mental formations.

a. Is it relevant in this moment?

No. Not at all.

b. Is it useful in this moment?

No. No way.

c. Is it conducive to peace in this moment?

No. It is just the opposite.

d. Am I out of it?

No. I want to be, but it is difficult.

II. *What are the feelings hidden in the dream?*

    a. What are the *causal feelings*? (State all the sets in the form of "I like that..." and "I dislike that...")

**I like that Lisa should not have insulted me.
I dislike that she did.**

**I like that Lisa should have apologized.
I dislike that she did not.**

**I like that our friendship should not have broken.
I dislike that it did.**

    b. What are the *consequential feelings*?

I am sad; sometimes angry; sometimes helpless. I cannot meditate and enjoy the moment.

    c. Do I want to be peaceful?

Yes. Nothing else is more important for me.

d. Keeping the causal feelings alive, can I attain peace?

No. I do want to give up my hopeless desires.

4. Carly understood that these two feelings could not remain together in the mind: desiring and peace. She decided to let go of her desires — her likings and dislikings. This was a big character shift in her life. She had made her first fruitful attempts at growing spiritually. When she finally made up her mind — and it was only a question of making up the mind — she felt "*so much relief.*"

5. Let us now go to the roots of desiring. Why do we have desires? Why do we like certain things and dislike others? If it causes us pain, why do we do that?

6. The simple answer is: *We do that because we want to be complete and happy. The equation "I + X = C" is at the root of desiring.* We have been unconsciously tutored by our society that we can attain completeness and happiness *only* when our desires get fulfilled. Actually, people in our world are so attached to this way of thinking that they have lost the ability to do the reality check.

We are all following each other in this blind alley of ignorance. We do not learn from the mistakes of others — nay, we do not learn even from our own mistakes.

7. This means that restlessness is due to desires and desires are due to our deep-seated want to be complete and happy. "I + X = C" is the second deeply embedded root. On reflection, Carly realized that the fulfillment of desires does not lead to lasting fulfillment in her. She does get temporary relief, but it does not last. "Desiring" continues to remain, as *the perspective that "dependence is necessary" does not change even when desires get fulfilled.* In reality, we are unwittingly creating more misery and turmoil in our lives by believing in the illusion of incompleteness.

8. The next profound question in the Deep Inquiry is asked in order to remove the illusion of incompleteness. We ask about the "I + X = C" equations and their consequences. As a result, we get detached from these equations and clear our way to freedom.

THE THIRD PROFOUND QUESTION

*"What are the incompleteness equations
hidden in the dream?"*

1. After applying the second question, we under-
    stand that likes-dislikes are the first roots of
    restlessness. We proceed further now to search
    for the roots of our likes-dislikes with the help
    of the third question:

III. *What are the incompleteness equations hidden in the dream?*

    You need to state all the equations in the form of "I +
    X = C." That is, replace X with your actual X factors
    and then ask yourself:

    a. If these desires get fulfilled, will I get
        lasting peace?
    b. What is my own history?
    c. Am I attaching myself with
        something permanent?
    d. Can incompleteness ever give completeness
        and freedom?

2. In answering the main question, you must come
    out with as many X-factor equations as there
    possibly are. Each dream thought might be

loaded with several of them that you are
normally unaware of.

3. You have already understood that you have
X factors because you believe that they
will give you fulfillment and happiness.
In reality, they only cause dissatisfaction.
Incompleteness can be removed only by
letting go of all the X factors.

4. The first subquestion, "If these desires get
fulfilled, will I get lasting peace?" makes
you understand that even when your desires
get fulfilled, you still remain unfulfilled as
you have other X factors in your life and
you are prone to having more in the days
to come. You can never get *lasting peace
or happiness* by the fulfillment of desires.
However, some temporary spurts of excitement do take place. They make you forget
your dissatisfaction for some time. But soon
afterward, you come back to the same old
state of incompleteness.

5. Your own life history always tells you that
in spite of the fulfillment of so many of
your desires, you are still unfulfilled. The
immediate proof of unfulfillment is that
you still have all these incompleteness equations alive in you. Your life to date consisted

of addicted shifting from one X factor
to another.

6. The first two subquestions take us to an
   infallible inference: *This is not the way.*
   Keeping the old perspective intact, it is
   not possible to experience lasting peace
   and happiness. Then what is the way out?
   It is not by remaining attached with the
   X factors, but by burning the X factory
   itself that you can get this sublime state of
   freedom. There is no other way.

7. The third subquestion makes us understand
   that the objects of desires are impermanent.
   The desires themselves are impermanent.
   The related feelings are impermanent.
   Then what is it that we are attaching
   ourselves with? And why?

8. Completeness has only one definition:
   CESSATION OF INCOMPLETENESS. The
   illusion that there must be dependence in
   order to become happy is the root cause
   of suffering. Unless you drop it and accept
   the state of completeness — unconditioned
   and without any dependence whatsoever
   — there is no hope. You will never be able
   to reach eternal joy and freedom using the
   beaten path.

9. How did Carly proceed further toward freedom? Study how she handles the third question:

III. What are the incompleteness equations hidden in the dream? (State all the equations in the form of "I + X = C" or "I + Y = IC" or "I – X = C" or "I – Y = IC," whichever is most appropriate.)

   i. **I + Lisa should not have insulted me = Completeness**

   I + Lisa insulted me = Incompleteness

   ii. **I + Lisa should have apologized = Completeness**

   I + Lisa did not apologize = Incompleteness

   iii. **I + Our friendship should not have broken = Completeness**

   I + Our friendship broke = Incompleteness

   a. If these desires get fulfilled, will I get lasting peace?

   No. I don't think so. When we were friends, I was not peaceful for certain other reasons. Even if Lisa apologizes, I don't think that that in itself is a sufficient reason for me to get lasting peace. However, I will feel good for some time, if she does that.

b. What is my own history?

I keep falling into similar traps of unhappiness, every now and then. This is not the first time in my life that a friend insulted me or a friendship broke. Initially, it hurts. But I continue living my life and after some time, I forget.

c. Am I attaching myself with something permanent?

Nothing is permanent in this world. Not even friendships! Nor these feelings!

d. Can incompleteness ever give completeness and freedom?

Never. I want to achieve inner completeness. I want to drop all my X factors!

10. We understand that closing the X-factor accounts one by one by the fulfillment of related desires is not the way to lasting peace and freedom. We now recognize that the only way is by burning the X factory itself — i.e., detachment from the possibility of falling into the trap of the illusion of incompleteness. It means we choose not to have any dependence whatsoever on anything external.

11. In the next chapter, we are going to study the roots of incompleteness equations.

Common Conditionings

Conditionings are general beliefs that
a group of people take to be absolutely true.

1. Why is it that in some countries, they abhor the
   idea of *living together* before marriage and in
   some others, it is a common way of life? Why is
   it that they hate people eating beef at one place
   and at another, it is normal to do so? Why do
   people have divergent cultures?

2. All societies have certain general beliefs that
   their people take to be absolutely true. There
   are certain *universal programs or conditionings*
   and there are some *local ones too*. When a child
   is born, it is fed with these conditionings from
   day one. The society or people around the child
   might not be doing it purposely, but it does
   happen unintentionally. As most of us live in
   unawareness of our thoughts, we cannot understand that we are getting conditioned. With
   time, we sincerely start feeling that our beliefs
   are absolute truths and we are not able to
   accept a mismatch of the beliefs with the reality.

Whenever such a conflict takes place,
pain results.

3. The conditionings are general beliefs and
whenever you are trying to figure out your
own ones, try to state them in an impersonal way. Some examples of *universal
conditionings* are:

a. Money gives happiness.
b. People should always love each other.
c. Good friendship should never end.
d. There should never be divorce.
e. Love should be reciprocated.
f. One should not get insulted in public.
g. One's good work should
get acknowledged.
h. Status and power give fulfillment.
i. One's love life should be respected
by others.
j. People should not interfere in others'
business.
k. Spiritual teachers should walk their talk.
l. Children should respect their parents.
m. Parents should always be there for
their children.
n. Parents should give space to
their children.
o. There should not be betrayal
in friendship.

p. There should not be adultery by one's partner.

q. Both parents should always bring up their children together.

r. Bosses should not scream.

s. Workers in a company should work hard and smart.

t. Good teams should always win.

u. Everybody should respect everybody else.

v. People should not steal.

w. There should not be war.

x. The environment should be respected.

y. Politicians should not be crooked.

z. Media should be responsible.

aa. There should not be problems in life.

ab. One should not fall sick/be sent to the hospital.

ac. There should be balance in all spheres of life.

ad. Truth should always prevail.

ae. Wives should be obedient and loving.

af. Husbands should listen to and take care of their wives.

ag. True love should always last.

ah. One should not be disturbed when one is sleeping.

ai. Beds should be comfortable.

aj. People's privacy should be respected.

ak. Bus rides should never be bumpy.

al. People should not ask
unnecessary questions.

am. Students in meditation retreats should
learn quickly.

an. People should not be obese.

4. *Some local conditionings* are:

 a. Meat eating is bad.

 b. One should not eat beef.

 c. One should not eat pigs.

 d. Children should not live with their
 parents when they become adults.

 e. Children should always live with
 their parents.

 f. Before marriage, lovers should not
 live together.

 g. Before marriage, lovers should
 live together.

 h. People should work hard for money.

 i. People should not give their lives
 for money.

 j. One should not keep the knife standing
 in butter.

 k. One's cap should not be put on
 the ground.

 l. A cat should not cross one's path.

5. These are the definitions of right-wrong,
good-bad, auspicious-inauspicious, etc.,
of groups of people like countries, tribes,

religions, cultures, and communities. For example, a group of people can believe that "there should not be *living together* before marriage as it is a corrupt practice." This general belief of the group is its conditioning that it unconsciously assumes to be an absolute truth. Another group of people may not believe in this notion. They rather believe that before making a commitment, one should live with one's partner for some time. It means that this belief is a relative notion and not an absolute one.

6. Generally, people don't understand the difference between an absolute truth and a relative notion. The latter can just be need based. When people mistakenly consider the relative as absolute, they frown, scorn, jeer, get upset, get depressed, commit crimes, and even commit suicide!

7. Desires and incompleteness equations get sculpted according to the conditionings. When one believes that "there should not be *living together* before marriage as it is a corrupt practice," one will naturally have a desire that one's near and dear ones should not go against this norm. If somebody breaks this rule, one gets angry or upset,

depending on the depth of the belief and
the type of relationship.

8. All conditionings are just some notions
that people take to be true. Societies create
them for their smooth running. But they
pay a big price when their people grow
miserable. As the mind consists of three
qualities and not just one, there will always
be big gaps between the beliefs and the
reality. People cannot always walk straight. It
is impossible. There will always be the pull
of Tamas and Rajas that will not let mind
get settled in Sattwa. But people are not
ready to accept that. Especially in the cases
of their near and dear ones, they are not
able to drop their conditioning-filled expectations. Hence they suffer.

9. At the current juncture in the history of
the world, most of its population belongs
to lethargy and sensuality. There is strong
attachment with conditionings and there
is hardly any possibility of detachment.
Spirituality — the work on the mind to
realize its highest possibility — is an objective science as it is based on certain solid
principles and the truths can be verified
by anybody. However, it is subjective also
as one has to be open to integrating the

learning in one's life. If one is always lost in thoughting and has no inclination to detach, i.e., if one really feels that one's beliefs are absolutely true, why will one try to come out of them? One will have no motivation to do so. Peace is not a priority for most people. And why should it be?!

10. For the sake of peace in yourself and in the society, you yourself will have to follow these norms. But if others are not following, you ought to understand them with a loving heart. The state of being free from all conditionings can happen to deserving individuals and not to groups of people. If somebody achieves that state, he or she will have perfect harmony with the flow of events. There will be unconditioned peace in the mind and loving gratitude in the heart. This is what they call "Freedom."

THE FOURTH PROFOUND QUESTION

"What are the general conditionings hidden in the dream?"

1. Why do you have incompleteness equations? What made you believe in them? In order to reach the roots of incompleteness equations, let us now take up the fourth profound question, which has five implication questions:

IV. *What are the general conditionings hidden in the dream?* (State all the conditionings in impersonal format and do the work on each one separately.)

    a. Is it reality?

    b. What is the reality?

    c. How do I feel when I am attached with this wrong notion?

    d. How do I feel if I detach from this wrong notion?

    e. What is preventing me from giving up this painful story?

2. "That people should always be respectful to each other" leads to "I + my friend should

respect me = Completeness/Happiness."
This desire for happiness leads to "I want
that my friends should not disrespect me"
and "I want that my friends should always
respect me." All these statements in quotes
are mere mental formations that you take
to be true. You hold them in the subconscious of the mind. As soon as something
contrary happens in your life, you suffer.
If something favorable happens, you feel
good. But it also makes you expect — which
means that you can be restless, edgy, and
scared that something adverse may happen
in the future.

3. There are two types of conditionings:

   a. *Should* conditionings — These have
   the following forms: "people *should* be
   compassionate," "love *should* be reciprocated," "there *should* not be problems in
   life," etc.

   b. *Unhappiness* conditionings — "money
   gives happiness," "attachment to children
   gives happiness," "fulfillment of desires
   gives happiness," etc. That is, "happiness
   comes from some external source."

4. Both these types always give unhappiness as
   they are absolutely not true — they don't
   always correspond to the reality. The reality

can be different and that is what causes suffering. If you are not adaptable to the reality of the world, you will live in pain. This pain can be there in the form of any of the consequential feelings. You might even have a very compassionate heart — but that is not sufficient for peace and fulfillment. If attaching with conditionings is pain, it clearly means that detachment from them is peace.

5. If you understand that these beliefs are just certain false ideas, and if you are a sane person, why will you not give them up? It is just these absurd mental formations that stop you from realizing your best potential! What does it cost to give them up?

6. The only person who can prevent you from detaching from a painful story is you. Do you still want to live in pain? Don't you see that your old ideas are stale and agonizing? Do you want to wake up now? Can you do it now?

7. When I first understood the Deep Inquiry, it was like the biggest revolution of my life. I was smiling at my age-old stupidities. How funny one can be!

8. Carly proceeded further with the Inquiry:

*IV. What are the general conditionings hidden in the
       dream?* (State all the conditionings and do
       the work on each one separately.)

Friends should respect each other.
**Friends should not insult each other; espe-
cially for no reason whatsoever.**

Good friendship should always remain.
**Good friendship should not have an abrupt
and bad end.**

**If a friend makes a mistake, she should
apologize.**
**Friends should not be callous toward each
other's feelings.**

Friendship gives happiness.

a. Is it reality?

No.

b. What is the reality?

Friends do insult friends.

Good friendships do break.

Friends are callous, sometimes.

**After hurting a friend, one may
not apologize.**

Friendship can cause pain also.

c. How do I feel when I am attached with these wrong notions?

Sad; sometimes angry; cannot enjoy the moment; cannot meditate.

d. How do I feel if I detach from these wrong notions?

I feel that a big load has been lifted off my head.

I feel light.

I can now understand Lisa.

I am in the moment now and wondering how a wrong notion can cause so many problems in one's mind.

I feel the flow of acceptance in my heart. It is soothing.

I feel free now. I understand that my happiness comes only from me.

e. What is preventing me from giving up this painful story?

Only I can stop me. I will not let that happen.

I want to accept. I don't want to resist the reality anymore and suffer.

9. Just see how damaging our stories can be! And how liberating it feels when you give them up! What is holding us back is our own mind. We need to detach from it in order to experience freedom. This is the sweetest possible living on the planet.

10. In the next chapter, we will come to know about a person who has been hindering our growth. It will be the revelation of a lifetime. Read the story attentively.

THE MIRROR

You are your own best friend.
You are your own worst enemy.

At the age of eighty, Swami Chinmay was made the abbot of
Atmananda Monastery. He had joined this monastery when he was
twenty years of age. He had seen the monastery grow from its humble
beginning to a worldwide phenomenon. Most of the previous abbots
had worked hard to create its branches in many big cities of the world.

Swami Chinmay was happy as well as unhappy over the expansion
spree. He was happy because there were millions who were benefiting
from the Vedantic teachings, but unhappy because for many monks,
this expansion itself had become the main goal of their lives. They
were ever busy in creating plans, asking for donations, and bringing
about impeccable executions. Swami Chinmay was seeing that over
years, Atmananda Monastery had imperceptibly moved from being a
spiritual organization to a business organization. The monks were
aggressive and ambitious. They hardly concentrated on their meditation and spiritual growth.

Swami wanted to bring about a change. He knew that if he did
not stop this mindless expansion, the monastery would meet the
same fate that many other spiritual organizations had met in the
previous centuries.

Swami made his first decision. He ordered the construction of Look-In Meditation Hall. Swami made an announcement that this hall was dedicated to a special deity who was most helpful for the sincere aspirants and most unhelpful to the insincere ones. The monks were not able to figure out whom their master was referring to. Some thought it would be Shani Devata and some others thought it would be Kuber. But they could not come to any clear understanding.

When the construction finished in six months, Swami convened a gathering of all the monks in the Look-In Meditation Hall. When they entered, they were surprised to find total darkness inside. There was only a small earthen lamp whose flame was too dim to see anything. Swami asked them to sit for meditation with their gaze fixed to the wall, below which the lamp was placed.

As the monks were looking at the blank wall in that dark room, they realized that it was not a wall. Slowly, some images started appearing before them. They got curious. Initially the images were hazy, but soon they became clear. The lamp was becoming brighter with every moment. Earlier, it had been deliberately kept at low flame. Now they could see themselves in what they had believed to be a wall. It was actually a huge wall-size mirror.

Then Swami explained: "In one's spiritual practice, one can have the company of a great teacher and one might also have studied many scriptures, but unless one befriends oneself, it is not possible to deepen the practice. Becoming one's own friend means loving oneself — nay one's Self — more than anything else in the world. Nothing else is real. Self is the only reality. If we remain lost in the whims, fancies, desires, expectations, and rest-lessness of the mind, it is not possible to experience the Self. The mind has to be stilled — only then this highest goal of human life can be attained.

"You are your best friend and you are also your worst enemy. When your thinking, speech, and activities are tuned to detach from your mind's restlessness and experience the Self, you are considered to be your best friend. But if you are over busy in fulfilling your desire-fed activities, your mind will lose all its subtlety and will not remain a good instrument for realizing its best possibility.

"The one you are seeing in the mirror is you yourself. You are the highest deity for yourself if you love yourself and do right contemplation and meditation. But the same can be your worst enemy if you remain lost in your restless mind. The choice is yours."

Then Swami Chinmay made it compulsory for all monks in his monastery as well as in all branches to sit for contemplation and meditation for at least two hours a day. Nobody was allowed to make any excuses. In the times of the Swami, Atmananda Monastery made brilliant spiritual progress as well. Everybody made excellent use of the mirror to look within.

1. You are the person who can hinder your progress by remaining attached with wrong beliefs. You are also the only person who can revolutionize your life. You are the only person who can influence your happiness

and your success. You are the only person who can help yourself. Your life will change when you will change and when you will decide to go beyond your limiting beliefs.

2. The most important relationship you can have is with yourself. Examine yourself, watch yourself. Don't be afraid of failures and losses. They come in your life to make you strong. They are like rocks to push so that you grow in endurance, fortitude, and equanimity. Do your best. Build yourself with deep contemplation and meditation. It's the way you face life that makes the difference.

THE FIFTH PROFOUND QUESTION

"Whose business?"

1. The fifth law of peace is "Pain is what you get when you step out of your own business." If you interfere in others' business and try to control them, you will suffer. But most of us feel that people, especially our relations, should be under our control. We have obsessive thoughts like these: "How can you accept your husband doing whatever he likes?"; "How can you accept your wife flirting with others?"; "How can you accept your children coming late from parties every day?"; "Is it not one's moral duty to try to control and bring people on the right path?"; "Is it not our ethical responsibility to criticize to keep relationships and society running smoothly?"

2. I would like to repeat what I have written before:

   a. Those who criticize are *always* found wanting in the same things that they criticize others about. Living in glass houses, they like throwing stones at others! When others do the same, they don't like it!

b. We also need to understand the difference between mindful compassion and impulsive interference. For example, in regard to your duty toward your children, your job is to provide the right environment and the best possibilities of growth. Of course, it is your dharma to give them the right guidance. But, the point is that even after having done your best, they may not follow what you think is the best course for them. *You will have to draw a line somewhere, lest your own life should get disturbed.* Similarly, in other relationships as well, the same needs to be followed. If your husband has decided to shift his commitment to somebody else, why do you still want to run after him? Bless him that he may find true fulfillment. Can you change his mind by using force or by getting angry? Don't you want to see him happy? His steps may not be conducive to realizing true happiness, but are yours conducive? Is he amenable to listening? You have to create such an inner environment that you remain balanced in all situations. Those who are going away, bless them. Those who are coming to you, help them. If you can do it, you will be a free person.

c. *Do your best, leave the rest.* While helping others, the chances that you may not get the desired response and your compassion may get misunderstood are always there. It is important to recognize the difference between interfering and living in compassion and peace. The former disturbs you and the latter gives you pure joy. In the second case, *you do your best without imposing any outcome.*

3. Both the *"should"* and *"unhappiness"* conditionings can be profited from. They are beneficial because they help us understand our business better. The fifth profound question has two subquestions too:

V. *Whose business?*

a. Am I stepping out of my own business and interfering?

b. What is my real business in this moment?

4. As you reflect and analyze further, you will undoubtedly realize that you were interfering in somebody else's business. What goes on in others' minds and how they behave is neither your business nor responsibility. *Nobody will change just because you want them to change. They will change only*

when they themselves will want to. They have
their own deep grooves of personality based
on the three qualities of the mind and their
X factors. *They sincerely feel that their path is
the best path for them.* Who are you to say that
they are wrong?

5. Will it not be a disservice if we shatter a
person's faith in his/her beliefs when he is
not ready to accept what we want to offer?
If yes, why are we offering? We also need to
ask ourselves if we are doing it with peace
and compassion or with an impulsive desire
that he should listen to us? Everybody is
acting compulsively, in a way. We have to
be aware that we don't do the same in the
name of love!

6. In the next chapter, we will learn how
to profit from our habits of judging
others and holding them responsible for
our uneasiness.

TURN-IN

Do unto others as you would have them do unto you.

1. For answering the second subquestion of the fifth one, "What is my real business in this moment?" do a self-analysis. **Turn-in** the *should* conditionings upon yourself. A turn-in means asking yourself if you are following those beliefs that you want others to follow.

2. There are two kinds of turn-ins. Let us try to understand them with this example:

   Suppose your conditioning is "people should respect each other." Then your turn-ins can be the following:

   a. *Me-first* turn-ins:

   "I should respect myself."

   "I should respect people."

   "I should respect the person from whom I am expecting respect."

   When you are doing the turn-ins, ask yourself, "Am I doing it in my life?" These turn-ins make you realize that you have to first live up to your beliefs in your own life. That is your main business. Not expecting anything from others and concentrating just on your own business shown by the turn-ins will immediately lead to the experience of *unconditioned peace.* You will understand what you are lacking in and your immediate business is to remove these lacunae from your mind. *You are no longer looking for scapegoats for your unhappiness.* You don't want to waste your energy in blaming and expecting. Rather, you now concentrate on your real responsibility of attaining unconditioned peace and fulfillment by letting go of your attachment with expectations.

b. *Acceptance* turn-ins:

"I accept that people can be disrespectful."

"I accept that my friend can be unaware."

This naturally leads to the understanding that nobody is to be blamed as there is an unconscious compulsion of personality that is deeply built in by nature and not by any humans. This turn-in will lead to the experience of *loving kindness for the person who you were blaming earlier.*

Unconditioned peace and love are your primary and foremost dharmas. If this state is achieved, your mind will be so much at ease and your heart will be full of kindness. You will start living your life moment by moment, day by day — full of peace and love. What more do you want? You will find yourself already there on the highest peak. Now, you just have to do practice for staying there.

3. It is not that after learning the Inquiry, your thoughting will cease completely. The previous character-patterns have a strong momentum that will keep creating turmoil in the mind. Whenever it happens, you will need to do the Deep Inquiry again. Each time you get lost, you will need to wake up again… and again… and again. Gradually, you will see that living on the highest peak will no longer remain a difficult job. You will, with consistent practice, create new grooves of understanding. Living in this freedom-perspective will become an effortless habit.

4. In regard to the unhappiness conditionings that are similar to the illusion of incompleteness, the turn-ins are very simple. For "Friendship gives happiness," the turn-ins are:

"I give myself happiness."

"Friendship may not always give happiness."

These turn-ins are meant to remind us that there is only one possibility of arriving at a state of freedom and completeness: cessation of incompleteness. That is, independence from all X factors. There is no other way.

THE LAST PROFOUND QUESTION

"Why should I give up my real business ever?"

1. Having experienced the state of freedom and having understood that this is your real business in this moment, ask yourself:

VI. Why should I give up my real business ever?

2. Once you are aware that your conditionings, incompleteness equations, and desires are harmful for you, why would you like to get trapped by them again? Unless you want it, they cannot get attached with you. You have to decide what kind of a life you want to live — peaceful, blissful, and loveful, or restless and painful. You will need to make a clear and decisive choice.

3. This choice is about *your life in totality*. What you practice and understand on your meditation seat will need to be practiced in the real life too. The differentiation between spiritual and secular ought not to remain for a sincere aspirant of freedom.

149.

4. Let me repeat this important point again:
   It is not that after doing the Deep Inquiry
   once, you will be free from your conditionings forever. The momentum of the past
   habit-patterns can cause restlessness again
   and you will have to patiently and systematically do the work again. It requires a
   life-long commitment. It needs agile awareness, all the time. Slowly and slowly, as you
   go on practicing, the new understanding
   will become stronger. You will need to have
   patience and keep practicing with serenity.
   There is no shortcut to freedom. And the
   rewards are priceless — you know that!

Six Profound Questions

I. Is it a dream or reality?

    a. Is it relevant in this moment?

    b. Is it useful in this moment?

    c. Is it conducive to peace in this moment?

    d. Am I out of it?

II. What are the feelings hidden in the dream?

    a. What are the causal feelings?

    b. What are the consequential feelings?

    c. Do I want to be peaceful?

    d. Keeping the causal feelings alive, can I attain peace?

III. What are the incompleteness equations hidden in the dream?

    a. If these desires get fulfilled, will I get lasting peace?

    b. What is my own history?

    c. Am I attaching myself with something permanent?

    d. Can incompleteness ever give completeness and freedom?

IV. What are the general conditionings hidden in the dream?

    a. Is it reality?

    b. What is the reality?

    c. How do I feel when I am attached with a
wrong notion?

    d. How do I feel if I am detached from the
wrong notion?

    e. What is preventing me from give up a
painful story?

V. *Whose business?*

    a. Am I stepping out of my business
and interfering?

    b. What is my real business in this moment?

VI. *Why should I give up my real business ever?*

In the next few chapters, we will do some case studies in
order to understand Deep Inquiry thoroughly.

Some Case Studies

John Mayor

What happens in a dream can very well happen in the waking state also. The way you react in the dream, you would do the same in your waking state as well. Remember John Mayor who had a dream about his suspicious wife, Nancy. In the dream, it reached a point where he wanted to file for divorce. Now, imagine that it was not a dream and it happened in reality. How would he do the Deep Inquiry?

Let us suppose that John is meditating on "This Moment, Mindful Moment." An agitation arises in his mind about his wife's strange behavior. When he comes out of the thoughting, his inquiry could be like this:

I. *Is it a dream or reality?*

> **I was experiencing my own thoughts and I was lost in them. It was a dream.**

    a. Is it relevant in this moment?

> **Only living in the moment is relevant.**

    b. Is it useful in this moment?

> **No. Just a futile dream. My wife will not change just because I want her to.**

    c. Is it conducive to peace in this moment?

    No. I am disturbed.

    d. Am I out of it?

    **Not really. I wish she did not behave
like that.**

II. *What are the feelings hidden in the dream?*

    a. What are the causal feelings?

    I like that Nancy trusts me.

    **I like that Nancy does not behave so
stupidly.**

    I want her to be happy.

    **I like to have a peaceful relationship with
Nancy.**

    **I dislike what she does and thinks, as it is
all nonsense.**

    b. What are the consequential feelings?

    I get angry.

    I feel like running away from her.

    **I start disliking her and my love for her
gets replaced by irritation.**

    I am sad.

    I cannot meditate.

    c. Do I want to be peaceful?

    Yes.

    d. Keeping the causal feelings alive, can I
attain peace?

    No. I need to weigh things clearly.

III. What are the incompleteness equations hidden in the dream?

I + sane Nancy = completeness and happiness

I + suspicious Nancy = incompleteness and unhappiness

a. If these desires get fulfilled, will I get lasting peace?

I don't think so. This is just one of the several accounts in my life. If this desire gets fulfilled, I have so many other issues hanging. When I had a good relationship with her, even then I was restless.

b. What is my own history?

Even when my desires get fulfilled, I remain unfulfilled as there is always something else.

c. Am I attaching myself with something permanent?

No. Nothing remains. The past situations have not remained. This one will also pass.

d. Can incompleteness ever give completeness and freedom?

Never. I only want inner completeness. Nothing less than that, whatever the cost.

IV. What are the general conditionings hidden in the dream?

Wives should not be suspicious.

Wives should not misunderstand husbands.

a. Is it reality?

No.

b. What is the reality?

Wives do misunderstand husbands. Wives can be suspicious.

c. How do I feel when I am attached with these wrong notions?

Angry. Sad. I feel I don't love her anymore.

But I do not want to feel like that. I want to be happy. I love her.

d. How do I feel if I detach from these wrong notions?

I can understand her attachment and possessiveness. She loves me and that makes her possessive.

I am more aware. I feel balanced and light.

e. What is preventing me from giving up these painful stories?

Nothing. I have given them up.

V. Whose business?

> *a.* Am I stepping out of my business and interfering?
>
> **How Nancy feels is her business.**
>
> **If I interfere in her business, I suffer. I don't want to suffer anymore.**
>
> *b.* What is my real business in this moment?
>
> **Me. Only me. I should understand my needs.**
>
> **I should be considerate to myself.**
>
> **I should understand Nancy's needs.**
>
> **I should understand human needs.**
>
> **I should understand the needs of people around me.**
>
> **I accept that wives may not understand husbands. There can be misunderstanding due to possessiveness.**
>
> **I accept it and I accept her as she is.**

VI. Why should I give up my real business ever?

> **No reason. I don't want to be sad and angry again.**

Susan Claire

Susan was unhappy with her job. It was a big burden for her to go to the office every day as she thought that her real passion was teaching kids. When she came to Z Meditation Centre to do the retreat, her whole being looked exhausted due to the work pressure.

She wanted to go back to her country with a clear mind. When Susan was doing meditation in order to understand and experience the bliss of the moment, these thoughts about her desire to change the job came and disturbed her. Then she did the Deep Inquiry.

I. *Is it a dream or reality?*

A dream. I am in India; I am not in the office now.

   a. Is it relevant in this moment?

   No. And yes also as I want to resolve it now.

   b. Is it useful in this moment?

   No. And yes. I want a solution.

   c. Is it conducive to peace in this moment?

   No. I am tired.

   d. Am I out of it?

   No. I want to resolve it once and for all.

II. What are the feelings hidden in the dream?

    a. What are the causal feelings?

        I like that I have passion for what I do.

        I dislike the routine office work.

        I want to live for kids. I love teaching.

        I don't want to go back to the office again.

    b. What are the consequential feelings?

        I am tired.

        I feel like a misfit in my office.

        I am also scared about my financial security if I leave my job.

        I am not able to enjoy this moment and what I have.

    c. Do I want to be peaceful?

        Yes. I want to be happy.

    d. Keeping the causal feelings alive, can I attain peace?

        No.

III. What are the incompleteness equations hidden in the dream?

    I + teaching kids = completeness and satisfaction

    I + going to office = incompleteness

    I + less pressure at work = happiness

    I + deadlines = unhappiness

a. If these desires get fulfilled, will I get lasting peace?

When I think about it, I realize that it has been a strong pattern in my life. Wherever I am, I am dissatisfied. Before I got the current job two years ago, I was unhappy and I desperately wanted to get this job. Now I am unhappy again.

b. What is my own history?

Same patterns keep repeating.

c. Am I attaching myself with something permanent?

No. The past had something else. The future will have something else.

d. Can incompleteness ever give completeness and freedom?

No. I understand that I will need to let go of my X factor. Only then can I be complete. I realize that it has also to do with all the troubles at the office. If it were an easy job, I wouldn't mind it so much.

Secondly, the salary is also not according to the work that I do. My company should be considerate.

It is actually a very complex situation.

IV. What are the general conditionings hidden in the dream?

All of one's desires should get fulfilled.

There should not be any problems in life.

There should be financial security.

The pay should be according to the work (pressure).

The employers should be considerate to the employees.

One should be able to do what one likes.

a. Is it reality?

No.

b. What is the reality?

These are just hopeless notions. The reality is just the opposite. My life is my greatest teacher of reality.

c. How do I feel when I am attached with these stories?

Exhausted. I just want to relax. I don't like anything. I am tired all the time.

d. How do I feel if I detach from these wrong notions?

I feel that I am standing aside and looking at my hopeless stories with detachment. I am mindful now. I have composure. I think I can confront my life with much more ease and balance.

e. What is preventing me from giving up these painful stories?

Only I can prevent myself. I don't want to do it anymore. But I also understand that there is a lot of work ahead.

V. *Whose business?*

a. Am I stepping out of my business and interfering?

I think it is my business in one way. But how things happen in life is not my business. My business is what I do with what happens in life.

b. What is my real business in this moment?

To live in the moment and enjoy it. The office problems and even the life problems can never be solved for good. Something will always remain unsolved. Some desires will not get fulfilled. Some will. This is the way. I accept it as it is. I am prepared to face my problems. I do think that I will like teaching kids more as that appears to be my dharma. But that is not important in this moment. I will need to make a thoughtful decision about this and I will do it when I go back. Right now, it is just this mindful moment that I am experiencing!

VI. Why should I give up my real business ever?

I want to live my life in awareness. There is no reason that I give up my freedom now.

Note: We need to differentiate between daydream agitations and conscious intelligent thinking. Walking on one's dharma ought to be a priority, no doubt. But just doing circles around this thought and remaining stressed about it is not good. First, attain peace by freeing yourself of conditionings. Then take your decisions wisely and prudently.

Did you notice how there was a shift from "passion for job" and "teaching kids" to "financial security," "pressure-free work," and "insufficient salary"? When you do the Inquiry, you are able to dig out your real attachments and fixations. Many times, they remain hidden behind a veil of dharma. That is, you actually want to fulfill your desires, but you want to have the solace that you are doing it for dharma.

Enat

Enat was disturbed that her mother was not well and was feeling very lonely in Israel. Enat was in the U.S. and had to take her exam the next day. She loved her mother and wanted to be with her ASAP. Therefore, she was not able to concentrate on her studies.

I. *Is it a dream or reality?*

A dream. My mind is overactive now. I am not able to control it.

   a. Is it relevant in this moment?

   No. I have my main exam tomorrow. It is important for me that I study.

   b. Is it useful in this moment?

   No. I can't go there now and I cannot concentrate also.

   c. Is it conducive to peace in this moment?

   No.

   d. Am I out of it?

   No. I love my mother. I can't see her suffering.

II. *What are the feelings hidden in the dream?*

   a. What are the causal feelings?

   I like to be with my mother when she needs me.

I dislike that she suffers and feels lonely.
I want her to be strong.

   b. What are the consequential feelings?
I feel helpless and sad.
I also feel lonely.

   c. Do I want to be peaceful?
Yes.

   d. Keeping the causal feelings alive, can I
attain peace?
No.
Does it mean that I detach myself from
my mother? It is difficult.

III. *What are the incompleteness equations hidden in the
dream?*

I + being with my mother = completeness
I − being with my mother = incompleteness

I + my mother consoled = completeness
I − my mother consoled = incompleteness

   a. If this desire gets fulfilled, will I get
lasting peace?
It will be a big relief for me, but it will
not give lasting peace, for sure. I know
that even when I am with my mother,
she has some reason or other to remain
unhappy. I have never been able to fulfill
all her wants.

b. What is my own history?

I am vulnerable to attracting the unhappiness of others. Not only my mother; when my friends are unhappy, I also become unhappy.

c. Am I attaching myself with something permanent?

No. Life's situations and problems keep changing. I also know that even if I don't go back to Israel now and explain my situation to her, she will understand and accept.

d. Can incompleteness ever give completeness and freedom?

No. Never. I want to be strong and complete within myself.

IV. What are the general conditionings hidden in the dream?

Mothers should not be too attached and miss their children. Mothers should not feel lonely.
Mothers should be wise and emotionally mature.

a. Is it reality?

No.

b. What is the reality?

Mothers are mothers. They are attached and dependent.

c. How do I feel when I am attached with these stories?

Sad. Very sad. And lonely. Helpless. Guilty.

d. How do I feel if I detach from these wrong notions?

Yes, these notions are wrong. I cannot help it. Mothers are what they are. If I detach from my stories, I feel light and peaceful. I can only do my best, but I cannot change mothers.

e. What is preventing me from giving up these painful stories?

I have already given them up as this is the most prudent choice for me.

V. *Whose business?*

a. Am I stepping out of my business and interfering?

Yes. I cannot help it.

b. What is my real business in this moment?

I should not miss myself by remaining lost in thoughting.

I should not miss my mother and be unhappy.

I should be wise and emotionally mature.
I should be happy and peaceful.
I should love myself.
I should love everybody.
I should love my mother as she is and not expect her to change overnight.
I should help my mother understand the conditionings, but if she does not, it's okay.

VI. Why should I give up my real business ever?

I feel light and free now. I don't want to feel guilty for no fault of mine. I love my mother. But I accept that mothers can be lonely sometimes. This is how they will learn and grow.
No reason to give up my real business ever.

Note: Enat needs to intelligently prioritize. Just living in agitation borne out of thoughtlessness is not good for her. She needs to create an inner peaceful environment first and then decide what she wants to do. She has to clearly and intelligently weigh between going back to Israel and living in the U.S. for her studies. Having come to whichever decision, she *should* live by it happily!

The Inquiry is leading to a state of understanding that wherever there are causal feelings, the consequential ones always follow. Wherever there are desires, some pain is always experienced. This is how nature helps us evolve from our current state of understanding. In other words, pain is not always bad. It might be necessary for the growth of the mind.

Carly

Carly did two Z Meditation Retreats back to back as she
felt that some remnants of conditionings were still left in
her mind. The following is her second attempt at Deep
Deconditioning Inquiry.

Carly was disturbed that Lisa insulted her. Lisa had a bad
relationship with her mother. She got angry with her one
day on the phone. When she came back to the room, she
started blasting Carly without any rhyme or reason. After
that, Carly left her and started living in a different place.
But the whole episode made her very angry and sad.
Now she was at the meditation center, trying to meditate.

I. *Is it a dream or reality?*
  Dream. A bad dream.

   a. Is it relevant in this moment?
     **No. Only living in the moment
     is relevant.**

   b. Is it useful in this moment?
     **No. Nothing is changing. Lisa will not
     accept that it was not right on her part to
     scream. And what she has done cannot
     be undone.**

   c. Is it conducive to peace in this moment?
     No. Not at all.

    d. Am I out of it?

    No and yes!

II. What are the feelings hidden in the dream?

    a. What are the causal feelings?

    I like that Lisa should not have insulted me.

    I dislike that she insulted me.

    I don't like the way our friendship ended.

    I would like Lisa to apologize.

    b. What are the consequential feelings?

    I am angry. The whole episode keeps running in my mind all the time.

    I also feel grateful to her sometimes when I remember the good times we had together. That makes me sad afterward.

    c. Do I want to be peaceful?

    That is what I want now.

    d. Keeping the causal feelings alive, can I attain peace?

    No. I need to prioritize. I know that if I have expectations, I will suffer.

III. What are the incompleteness equations hidden in the dream?

    I + Lisa should not have insulted me = completeness

    I + Lisa's insults = incompleteness

    I + Lisa feeling sorry = completeness

    I + unapologetic Lisa = incompleteness

a. If these desires get fulfilled, will you get lasting peace?

No, I don't think so.

b. What is my own history?

I think I somehow attract such a behavior from my friends. More often than not, they start taking me for granted. In this case also, Lisa was angry with her mother. It had nothing to do with me. But she chose to vomit all her anger on me. Perhaps, I need to learn my lesson finally. Perhaps, I need to be strong and people around me should not get this message that I can be easily walked over.

c. Are you attaching yourself with something permanent?

In a way, no. This incident is over, I understand. If I keep expecting, I will suffer. But my lessons should always remain with me. I also accept that there are more important things in life than getting angry over somebody's behavior.

d. Can incompleteness ever give completeness and freedom?

No. I want to drop my X factor for good. Let the world do whatever, I should still be able to remain indifferent and peaceful.

IV. *What are the general conditionings hidden in the dream?*

Friends should respect each other.

Friends should not insult each other.

Friendships should last.

There should not be an abrupt end to a good friendship.

People should not vomit their poison on friends.

a. Is it reality?

No. I wish it were all true. But it is sad that it is not true.

b. What is the reality?

Friends can be callous. Friends can be lethargic.

c. How do I feel when I am attached with these stories?

Angry and sad. Helpless also.

d. How do I feel if I detach from these wrong notions?

These notions have been very dear to me all my life and I have suffered a lot due to them. Not anymore. I need grounding in reality. If I detach, I feel I can understand people better. Why they do what they do — that is clear to me now. I can accept that people and even friends can be insulting, sometimes. They have their

X factors which make them behave so
callously. It's okay. I feel compassion
for Lisa. I feel silence and kindness in
my being.

e. What is preventing me from giving up
the painful stories?
**I am detached and I am free. I don't
want to give up my freedom now.**

V. *Whose business?*

a. Am I stepping out of my business and
interfering?
**Yes. How Lisa behaves is her business.
How people behave is their business.**

b. What is my real business in this moment?
**I should respect myself. My peace of
mind is my respect for myself.
I should not insult myself by becoming
angry and sad.
I should respect Lisa and understand her.
I should not insult Lisa by getting angry
with her — even in my mind.
My love for myself should last.
I accept that nothing lasts, not even
friendships.
I understand that anything can end
abruptly. I should be prepared for every-
thing.
It is okay that some people need to vomit**

**out in order to feel light.
I should not vomit and instead, I should
do Deep Inquiry.**

VI. Why should I give up my real business ever?

**I want to be free. Always. I don't want
to give up this state of understanding
and compassion.**

Note: You have learned how to apply Deep
Inquiry on your restlessness. Now, take up
your major thoughting and do the whole
work in writing.

In the next chapters, we will be taking up some questions
that were asked during the meditation retreats.

QUESTIONS

Q. Why meditation?

A. To become mindful, peaceful, blissful, and loveful. To experience the joy of freedom from the restlessness of mind. To know the Self.

Q. I am quite conscious of myself. I can do investigation when I am agitated. What is so unique about meditation?

A. Becoming conscious in this manner is the first step. The next step is to be conscious of the perspective that leads to agitation. Are you aware of your perspectives?

Q. What do you mean by that?

A. Does your happiness come from within you or from outside — from yourself or from people and situations?

Q. It comes from within me, I know. But when I am agitated, I think that it is due to external factors.

A. It means that the seeds of right understanding are there, but they are not strong enough. They need to sprout now.

Q. How do you do that?

A. By meditation. Meditation means correcting your wrong perspective and applying the truth to your real life. Please understand that meditation is not just a routine tool that you may use in times of distress. It is about your whole life — straightening your priorities, removing the illusions, finding the truth, living in equanimity and inner joy.

WHAT IS THE RIGHT ATTITUDE FOR MEDITATION?

Q. I never knew that it was due to involuntary thoughts that I was not able to meditate. Please tell me what is the right attitude for meditation?

A. It is so beautiful that you have realized that your own mind creates obstacles. Your happiness and unhappiness do not come from outside. In order to realize the state of *stable blissful awareness*, all the illusion-holes in the mind need to be plugged. Dependence is the biggest hole. You need to be ruthless in the practice as you will see that your mind will play tricks and try to deceive you in many ways.

Keep in mind these four important points:

a. Courage in the wake of all adverse opinions. Others may not understand you. It is okay. You have to understand them and not try to impose your views on them.

b. Indifference to your agitations born out of false notions. You have to have a very sincere desire to drop the long-cherished stories of your mind. Let yourself not get duped by your own mind. It is still like a young sapling. You will also need to protect it cautiously.

c. Keep the flame of love for yourself alive, even if you fail once in a while.

d. Have a discipline of regular and systematic meditation. Go on working on yourself until living in your divine nature becomes natural and effortless for you.

Q. I understand the whole process, but it looks like a very difficult task.

A. Take your steps. Just do it. The hike to the top of a mountain begins with the first step and then you go on advancing step by step. You must start doing the practice diligently and regularly. You also have to understand that your direction should be right. Whatever meditation practice you adopt for yourself, it ought to have detachment and right understanding as its main ingredients.

If the heart is already loving, why should one
meditate?

Q. What do you say of people who are already very loving
and considerate to others? Why should they meditate?

A. Are they peaceful too? Do they have equanimity, whatever the situations are? Do they experience inner
fulfillment or do they still live in the illusion that
happiness and completeness come from outside?

Compassionate state is the fourth state on the ladder
of evolution. My experience is that it is a lovely state to
be in, but it is not the end of the game. It is rather the
beginning of spirituality.

Most of the students who get interested in meditation
retreats like Z Meditation belong to the compassionate
state of being. They are wonderful people, but restless.
They suffer due to various illusions of understanding.
If they want to be peaceful, they need to have a good
grounding in the right knowledge.

Q. If one has a clear direction about dharma — what one
should do in life — should one meditate even then?

A. You are still concentrating on the externals. You are
still believing that happiness comes from outside. This
is wrong thinking.

Knowing one's dharma in this sense only means that
you understand what ought to be your calling or vocation. That is a necessary step. You will be comparatively

happy going to your workplace. You will have less disturbing thoughts, at least on this account.

Is that the end of life? Are you living just for doing a certain work? Have you realized lasting fulfillment and is your mind peaceful? If yes, you do not need to meditate. If no, you still need to remove the illusions of understanding and realize the inner bliss. How can that be possible without meditation?

WHY SO MUCH THINKING IN MEDITATION?

Q. If one has to go beyond thinking, why do you put so much emphasis on thinking?

A. Meditation is a three-step process:

  a. You listen to the Truth.
  b. You contemplate on it.
  c. You have deep meditation.

If you look at the ladder of evolution, you will appreciate that most people in the world are still hovering around sensuality and lethargy. If such minds sit for meditation without having a clear discipline of contemplation, they are bound to fail.

As you climb the ladder, the mind gets less and less chaotic. But chaos cannot be completely removed without removing the illusions. Happiness-coming-from-outside is the basic misunderstanding of most minds. Unless you remove it, there is no possibility that your mind will attain peace as it will keep projecting the related agitations.

How will you remove your involuntary dreaming without removing the illusions of understanding? How can you remove illusions without contemplating deeply on the nature of reality? Contemplation is a necessary step in meditation.

If you want to remove a thorn from your finger, you need another thorn to take out the first one. Later on, you throw both of them away. When contemplation will become deep, you will naturally be peaceful and blissful. There will not be much thinking required then. Until then, it is imperative.

Please understand that I am encouraging you to do contemplation right now. It will help in removing the thorns of wrong understanding. It will naturally develop into effortless meditation when you attain maturity.

I am not able to agree with those who propound the practice of mindlessness or thoughtlessness in the beginning itself. It is not possible to do that for the novices. **The higher mind needs to be used to gobble the lower mind.** *Using the right understanding, one has to remove the wrong understanding.* Hence, contemplation or right thinking in meditation is encouraged.

RELIEF OR CURE?

Q. I am a marathon runner. The state of bliss that you are talking about is attained in long-distance running also. How is it different from meditation?

A. Relief or Cure — what is the goal? It is true that you can attain relief from your mind by running or by doing yogic postures or by some breathing exercises. But these efforts do not change your perspective. The wrong beliefs still remain active in the background.

In your computer, there are so many programs that run in the background, e.g., the virus-removal program, the speed-enhancer program, etc. You might not be aware that they are active in your computer, but they keep doing their jobs. Similarly, there are programs that keep running in the background of the mind, too. You don't become aware of them unless you turn your gaze toward them.

If these mental programs are based on wrong notions, they will give you a lot of pain eventually. Even when they are not giving you pain, they do result in excessive restlessness. You cannot remove this state of being just by running a marathon. You will have to bring about corrections in your thinking process.

Moreover, how long can you run? What after that? We have devised countless ways to delay facing ourselves! We watch TV or go for a picnic or have endless daily chores. We create such activities because we do not want to face ourselves. If we have nothing to do, we get bored and look for avenues so that we may keep running away from ourselves. Please understand that nothing external will give lasting happiness. It is impossible!

I ask you the question again. What do you want — a relief or a cure?

IS LASTING PEACE POSSIBLE?

Q. Do you think that in the hectic Western world, it is possible to attain lasting peace of mind?

A. It is in this hectic world that I see greater possibility of attaining peace. If you observe closely, you will see many openings. There are so many people in the West who are getting fed up with sensual living. There are communities catering to the growth of compassion and self-awareness. People love helping others. There is a growing demand for self-growth and spirituality. Don't you see how many millions of such books are read by people in the Western world? A marvelous revolution of understanding is happening here. I can see that in the next step of evolution, there is going to be more and more desire to realize the inner bliss. If it will not happen here, it cannot happen anywhere.

Q. Don't you think that it is difficult to meditate in such a hysterical life?

A. I am hearing that you are asking the question about yourself and not about the entire Western world. It is no doubt difficult, but who will sort things out for you? Who will do the prioritization for you? Think of the person at a seashore waiting for all the waves to subside before he would jump in the waters for swimming. Is it ever possible?

First of all, decide what you want from your life. If an angel appears to you now and gives you one boon, what would you ask for? Why? Do you want to be in command of your life? Do you want freedom more than anything else? If yes, you will not be asking this question again. You will get going on this path of inner fulfillment and bliss.

Will meditation impede creativity?

Q. What about creativity? Stopping the dreams will affect creativity and intuitions. Will it not?

A. The flow of creativity needs to be differentiated from chaotic agitations of the mind. When the mind is restful, there is not only better concentration on the job at hand, there is also a better possibility of the flow of creative and intuitive thoughts. The more the chaos, the less this is possible. All great creative works were created by focused minds and not by chaotic and confused minds.

Q. How about planning for the future and learning from your past mistakes? Is that the same as living in the future or past?

A. Here also, try to understand the difference between conscious voluntary thinking and unconscious involuntary thoughting. Thinking is very different from running in circles. The former is to be encouraged as it gives you a direction and it helps you grow. The latter is futile in every sense. It just dissipates your energies.

Conscious thinking about the past and the future is actually necessary for most of us as it helps in giving our lives a positive direction. It helps in keeping one fruitfully busy. Otherwise, a great deal of lethargy can creep in the mind. It has happened with many practitioners. Be careful.

Q. Does meditation help in arriving at big life-decisions?

A. Indecisiveness is due to the agitations of the mind caused by attachment with X factors. It happens when you are confused about a certain issue. You are not able to weigh the pros and cons clearly. It results in a glut of unmanageable involuntary dreams that hamper the exercise of volition.

With meditation, you will strengthen the mind. With the removal of chaos, dilemmas, and confusions, you will have mental clarity and decision-making will become easier.

MEDITATION CAN BE SCARY. I DON'T WANT TO FACE
MYSELF.

Q. Going to meditation and facing oneself is scary. I
don't want to do that. Is it not better to keep living
in darkness?

A. You can of course continue living the way you want.
Nobody can stop you from running away from yourself. But why do you want to do that? I don't think it
serves any purpose at all.

What I understand from your question is that you don't
want to confront the truth that you need to be independent of your sweet crutches — your attachments.
You like the illusion that others will make you happy.
You dislike any tinkering with your imaginary cocoons.

Pigeons close their eyes when they face cats pouncing
on them. They are too scared to face the reality. But
closing the eyes will not solve the problem of big cats
in your mind. Where can you run away from them?

Unless the right understanding dawns, the fears
cannot be overcome. Face your fears. They are just
absurd stories. If you want happiness in your life —
and I am seeing that there is a severe dearth of it right
now — you will have to confront both your problems
and yourself. Running away or shoving things under
the carpet is never a solution.

Q. When you talk of controlling the mind, do you mean it as a way of life?

A. Yes. How can you know a certain truth in your meditation and forget it completely when you get up from the seat of meditation? Meditation will never deepen if there is lack of integration with real life.

WILL MEDITATION HELP ME IN MY EXAMS?

Q. I am studying for my degree. How do I apply these concepts?

A. When you study, do thoughts about the future haunt you — "Will I get good grades?," "Will I get a good job?," and similar concerns about what comes next?

Q. Yes, all the time. But that is natural.

A. Yes, in a way. Don't you think that you have a fixed amount of mental energy and a lot of it gets wasted in futile daydreaming like that? Imagine putting yourself wholeheartedly into the present moment and studying. Won't your concentration be better and therefore your grades also?

Involuntary dreams don't take you anywhere. You just fritter away your energies and become unhappy. Your efficiency suffers at the same time. Is it a happy state of being?

Q. But the thoughts of the fruits come on their own.

A. That is fine. Don't worry about what you don't create deliberately. You just do your conscious work on removing the wrong notions from your mind. Gradually, this restlessness will fade away on its own.

Secondly, having dreams of fruits does not ensure their materialization in any way. But, if you have a restful frame of mind and better concentration, there is a healthy possibility that you will be able to achieve them.

How do I know my current state of evolution?

Q. How do I know which state of consciousness I am in?

A. Find out your X factors. When you try to meditate, what kind of dreams do you get?

If your dependence is on gossiping, alcohol, drugs, TV, etc., and if you like procrastinating, blaming, criticizing, and not taking responsibilities, you may be in the lethargic state of consciousness. If, however, you are driven by money, attachment with people, sex, and status, you may be in the sensual state. If you get enchanted by creativity, it is the creative state. If, on the other hand, you love helping people or other beings and want to see them come out of their suffering, it is the state of compassion. If you like meditating and are working to attain a state of unconditioned happiness and love, you may be in the state of introspection. When you reach the last two states, all objects of dependence are dropped and you are naturally staying in the state of eternal blissful awareness as this is realized to be your true identity.

Q. But I find myself oscillating between the first five. What should I do?

A. That is beautiful. You have all the potential for attaining freedom. Try to spend more and more of your conscious time in the states of introspection and compassion. You will need to make an effort for that as the pull of the senses and lethargy are still there. It is like working against gravity. With consistent and systematic practice, you will be able to stay in peaceful awareness effortlessly.

CAN YOU AVOID WORRYING?

Q. I worry a lot and I think you cannot avoid certain worries like when your child is sick.

A. I think it is not the sickness of the child that gives you worry; it is rather the sickness of *"your"* child that causes worry. Nature has created the notion of possession and the consequent suffering associated with it. Nature has also created the possibility of understanding that all notions are transitory mental formations. It is possible to live in the state of pure awareness and selfless love at the same time. The question is whether you want to do that or not and if you are ready for that state of pure being or not.

Q. I think I want to reach there, but it appears to be difficult. I love my child.... Can you please tell me the difference between love and attachment?

A. When your love is free from desires and expectations, it is love at its best — love just for its own sake. When there are expectations, it is attachment and it causes suffering in the long run. I am not saying that attachment is bad or wrong. I think it is also a wonderful feeling. The love of a mother for her child — wow! I wish I had an iota of that love in my heart. It is amazing to me; it is brilliant. But the only cause of alarm is that most mothers in this world are unhappy.

Can mothers do something to achieve this state of freedom? I think, yes. It is just a matter of fixing the gaze on this goal and doing deep contemplation to achieve it.

CAN YOU EVER DO YOUR JOB WITH PASSION IF YOU DO NOT WORRY AT ALL?

Q. I am a manager in an aviation company in England. I have learned that if you don't worry, you cannot do your job with passion.

A. Indirectly, what they have taught you is that unless you are whipped, you cannot work. Why do you always need the mental flogging given by desires, ambitions, and achievements to get going? Most people in the world do need this kind of a life as there are countless desires whose fulfillment is their sole goal. Hence, in order to cater to such a mindset, our schools impart such teachings.

However, for those who want mental peace, it can be counterproductive. One cannot become a worried free man! It is absurd. For such people, the requirement is to work with *awareness, happiness, and love* in their heart — doing everything with enjoyment.

I also think that your productivity increases as you attain balance of mind. When there is less dissipation of mental energies, you will give better results. That is, you will become a happy and more efficient worker. Your decision-making abilities are also honed when there is enjoyment and freedom in the heart. Your work does not remain a routine boring job for you anymore. You look forward to going to work, every day.

I am also not in favor of sacrificing the peace of individuals for the sake of profits of companies. The companies ought to be proactive in encouraging their employees to lead happy lives. In this way, workers will be able to serve the companies better.

I AM IN LOVE WITH SOMEBODY ELSE'S GIRL.
WHAT SHOULD I DO?

Q. I met a girl a few days before coming to the retreat. We sat together for some time in a room. We felt that both of us were gods and were transferring energy to each other. This girl has a boyfriend, but I think that she is now attracted to me. I am in a dilemma. I am not able to concentrate in meditation. What should I do?

A. Let go.

Some of us have a strange habit of divinizing mundane desires in order to justify them. What I can clearly see in this case is the mental monkeys playing their antics. Come back to the basics — she cannot give you lasting fulfillment and you also cannot give her the same. "I + X = C" is an illusion. The whole thing might end up in remorse and quarrels.

Secondly, don't do unto others what you don't want them to do to you. I am sure you don't like getting cheated?

Q. Who likes that?

A. Apply the same standards to yourself that you apply to others.

Q. But there are certain things that give satisfaction.

A. The main problem of the world is this "*but.*" You know a certain thing to be true, but you don't want to apply it — your desires get in the way.

Your need is to learn how to balance your feelings with right understanding. This world will become a chaotic place if everybody just follows his desires without considering the effects.

If you don't want to suffer later on, always think of the long-term consequences. Please understand that what gives you satisfaction today may become a problem tomorrow. Your solutions can turn into troubles in due course.

How can one be happy without desires?

Q. Without desires and their fulfillment, I don't understand the concept of happiness.

A. Do you want to say that having desires and then trying to fulfill them gives you a sense of fulfillment?

Q. Yes.

A. Is it *desiring* that gives fulfillment or the fulfillment of those desires?

Q. The desires keep me going and their fulfillment gives me fulfillment.

A. It means that you feel unfulfilled without the fulfillment of desires. Suppose you have one hundred years to live. How much time do you think you would give to desiring and working for their fulfillment and how much to the enjoyment of fulfillment?

Q. I think most of my time is spent in working and chasing. I understand what you want to say.

A. What I am asking is why can't you start from the state of fulfillment itself? When you *believe* that you must desire in order to get fulfilled and happy, you are unconsciously accepting that your fulfillment will come from external objects. It cannot. It never does *come* from anywhere. You have just created an imaginary void within yourself and now you want to get rid of it. You first make yourself *believe* that there is a void and you are conditioned to fill it up using temporary external means. Even when your desires get fulfilled, you still remain unfulfilled because this illusion of *first unfulfillment and then fulfillment* is still active in you. It will make you chase something else. It goes on until you pass away one day.

DO YOU WANT US TO BECOME MONKS?

Q. Do you want us to become monks?

A. Yes and no. It depends on how you define a monk. If a monk is one who lives by right understanding, yes. If a monk is one who lives in a forest or a monastery, no.

I understand you believe in the illusion that your happiness is dependent upon others. I am encouraging you to think about it deeply and if, even after that, your belief is sustained, go on living the way you have been living. Just learn to think. Don't believe in what others make you think.

Q. I may be wrong, but I also feel that I will become like a cabbage if I follow you.

A. Well, how do you define a cabbage?

Q. It does not feel. It cannot love.

A. Do you think a Buddha does not love? I repeat that you need to do deep thinking. When you achieve inner fulfillment and freedom, how will you spend your time? You can never become callous. Your whole being will be full of love. You will of course be free from desires and expectations. There will be no heartbreaks for you.

I only ask you to question your beliefs. If you do it in the right spirit, you will surely be free from suffering. It cannot be that you live in harmony with truth and be unhappy also. It cannot be that you live free from illusions and live like a cabbage. You will be a source of love and peace for whosoever comes in contact with you.

When you meditate, you learn to sublimate your feelings. You move from desiring to accepting, from attachment to love; from greed to contentment. You grow toward peace and freedom. Your Tamasic-Rajasic feelings give way to Sattwic ones. You do not become a cabbage. You rather become a source of love and joy for people around you.

Are all desires bad?

Q. Are all desires bad?

A. Desires are desires. The consequences can be painful. You need to decide what is good and bad *for you*. These are relative terms. If being happy and fulfilled is good for you, desiring will not be helpful.

Q. I just want good concentration. Raising the level of consciousness is not what I want. I want to have desires.

A. That is perfect for you. Please do the "This Moment, Mindful Moment" exercise with the breath. It will be helpful.

Q. I also think that you are brainwashing our minds.

A. You are right. I am washing the brains of wrong notions. Is it something bad, in your view?

Q. Well, we need to think on our own.

A. Precisely. This is exactly what I am also asking you to do. Don't follow anyone else. The society might have unconsciously injected several programs in your mind. I am only asking you to detach from them and find out for yourself if they are good for you or not. If they are good, go on living in them. But if you attain clarity that they are not good for you, have the courage to detach.

I am only teaching you how to ask right questions and how to find out what is hidden inside of you. I do not tell you the answers of the Deep Inquiry. That is what you need to get on your own. I want that you be objective in your thinking and in answering the questions. Drop all your previous stories and then answer the questions from your heart. In my view "thinking on one's own" means objective thinking and not biased thinking.

Please understand that I only want you to blossom. I have nothing personal to gain from the work. It is for your good that you need to do it.

HOW Z MEDITATION
CHANGES LIVES

I was suffering from depression and having a hard time breaking free. The Z Meditation inquiry method helped me to understand my conditionings and attachments and to think clearly. It made me aware that I was not primarily my mind, my emotions, nor my physical body, but so much more... My life is now full of beautiful experiences, opportunities, acceptance, and love. I finally feel peaceful and whole. — DARCEY DONOVAN

Upon arrival to [Ajay's] retreat there was an immediate overwhelming sense of peace and comfort that made me feel very secure about what would take place in the coming two weeks.... I realized there are no problems, there are no worries, I am not my future, I am not my past, nor am I my personality traits. I realized that the only thing that truly matters is this single moment. And that this single moment, without all the preconceived notions — is perfect. These last four years, since first encountering the Deep Inquiry and Deconditioning techniques, have been the most peaceful of my life. Even as I work in a field that requires me to see so much negativity of the world every single day, my heart is still filled with love and joy. — JESSIKA AVA

I have tried multiple meditation techniques, and *Free Your Mind* is by far the most powerful and most accessible form of meditation I have tried.... Taught incrementally, each step of the deconditioning process bares its own purpose, settling any discomfort or trepidation the student might face while learning the technique. I highly recommend the meditation technique that Ajay has dutifully developed for the betterment of personal relations with the Self, others, and society at large. — TARA CELENTANO

[*Free Your Mind* is] much more than a course in meditation; it changed my life completely. — LEE SOK LIAN

[Ajay's teachings helped me] to "Wake Up," open my self and my soul, and become "Aware" through the practice of meditation, yoga, and mindfulness and the joy of "Living in the Now." — ANNE

FURTHER QUESTIONS AND INQUIRY

For questions about deepening your meditation experience, please contact *ajay@zmeditation.com.*

For information about doing Z Meditation Retreats go to *www.zmeditation.com* or contact *suruchi@zmeditation.com*

ABOUT THE AUTHOR

There are two aspects in anybody's life:

    a. **The externals:** When was one born? From
    where did one graduate? Where did one do
    one's jobs?

    b. **The internals:** How did one live one's life?
    What were the guiding principles? How
    strong was one in following those principles?

Ajay Kapoor feels that the first aspect is banal and inconsequential. It is the second one that is really important for him.
From this perspective, he wants to share his guiding principles, upon which he is making sincere efforts to establish
his life.

They are:

a. The only goal worth pursuing in this
finite and restless life is the realization of
the eternal blissful Self that is the source
and substance of all that is.

b. This sublime goal can only be achieved by
stilling the mind. On stillness, an experience of one's identity with the absolute
Self automatically takes place.

c. Stillness of mind cannot be achieved if
there are desires, expectations, and conditionings that always lead to restlessness
and pain. In other words, an unhappy
mind cannot even appreciate the possibility of stillness, much less experience it.

d. It is not sufficient to merely gain spiritual knowledge. Unless one practices it,
assimilates it, and lives it, one cannot
gain stability. Without stability, there is
no possibility of stilling the mind and
attaining the Self.

Ajay has been teaching these principles in Z Meditation
silent retreats in Dharamsala, India. Thousands have
understood and benefited. This book is an effort to reach
out to those who cannot come to India to learn and practice. In due course, if Universe wills, there will be a few
more books that will help in consolidating what has been
learned in this first book.

ABOUT THE AUTHOR

HERE ARE OTHER **DIVINE ARTS** BOOKS YOU MAY ENJOY

DIVINE
ARTS

THE SACRED SITES OF THE DALAI LAMAS
Glenn H. Mullin   2013 Nautilus Silver Medalist

"As this most beautiful book reveals, the Dalai Lamas continue to teach us that there are, indeed, other ways of thinking, other ways of being, other ways of orienting ourselves in social, spiritual, and ecological space.."
— **Wade Davis, Explorer-in-Residence, National Geographic Society**

THE SHAMAN & AYAHUASCA: *Journeys to Sacred Realms*
Don José Campos   2013 Nautilus Silver Medalist

"This remarkable and beautiful book suggests a path back to understanding the profound healing and spiritual powers that are here for us in the plant world. This extraordinary book shows a way toward reawakening our respect for the natural world, and thus for ourselves."
— **John Robbins, author, *The Food Revolution* and *Diet for a New America***

A HEART BLOWN OPEN: *The Life & Practice of Zen Master Jun Po Denis Kelly Roshi*
Keith Martin-Smith   2013 Nautilus Silver Medalist

"This is the story of our time... an absolute must-read for anyone with even a passing interest in human evolution..."
— **Ken Wilber, author, *Integral Spirituality***

"This is the legendary story of an inspiring teacher that mirrors the journey of many contemporary Western seekers."
— **Alex Grey, artist and author of *Transfigurations***

SOPHIA—THE FEMININE FACE OF GOD: *Nine Heart Paths to Healing and Abundance*
Karen Speerstra   2013 Nautilus Gold Medalist

"Karen Speerstra shows us most compellingly that when we open our hearts, we discover the wisdom of the Feminine all around us. A totally refreshing exploration, and beautifully researched read."
— **Michael Cecil, author, *Living at the Heart of Creation***

NEW BELIEFS NEW BRAIN: *Free Yourself from Stress and Fear*
Lisa Wimberger

"Lisa Wimberger has earned the right, through trial by fire, to be regarded as a rising star among meditation teachers. No matter where you are in your journey, New Beliefs, New Brain will shine a light on your path."
— **Marianne Williamson, author, *A Return to Love* and *Everyday Grace***

1.800.833.5738   24 HOURS

ENERGY WARRIORS: *Overcoming Cancer and Crisis with the Power of Qigong*
Bob Ellal and Lawrence Tan

"The combination of Ellal's extraordinary true story and Master Tan's depth of knowledge about the relationship between martial arts and wellness makes for a unique and important contribution to the growing body of literature about holistic thinking and living."
— Jean Benedict Raffa, author, *Healing the Sacred Divide* and *The Bridge to Wholeness*

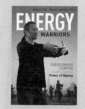

A FULLER VIEW: *Buckminster Fuller's Vision of Hope and Abundance for All*
L. Steven Sieden

"This book elucidates Buckminster Fuller's thinking, honors his spirit, and creates an enthusiasm for continuing his work."
— Marianne Williamson, author, *Return To Love* and *Healing the Soul of America*

2500 YEARS OF WISDOM: *Sayings of the Great Masters*
D.W. Brown

The wisdom of the greatest minds on earth. All in one place.
This book of carefully selected and arranged quotations represents the greatest philosophical thoughts mankind has produced in its attempt to come to a deeper understanding of the human condition.

WRITING FROM THE INSIDE OUT: *The Practice of Freeform Writing*
Stephen Lloyd Webber

"I urge others to write from the heart to find their true artistic voice. Here is a book that profoundly helps one explore that mysterious personal journey. A navigation guide to our inner creative magic."
— Pen Densham, screenwriter, *Robin Hood: Prince of Thieves* and *Moll Flanders*

CHANGE YOUR STORY, CHANGE YOUR LIFE: *A Path to Success*
Jen Grisanti

"It turns out you can actually get a handle on your life problems by approaching them as an ongoing story that you can rewrite and direct for a better effect."
— Christopher Vogler, author, *The Writer's Journey*

HEAL YOUR SELF WITH WRITING
Catherine Ann Jones

"An elixir for the soul"
— *Psychology Today*

"This is so much more than a book on writing. It is a guide to the soul's journey, with Catherine Ann Jones as a compassionate teacher and wise companion along the way."
— Dr. Betty Sue Flowers, Series Consultant/Editor, *Joseph Campbell and the Power of Myth*

DIVINE
RICHMOND HILL
PUBLIC LIBRARY

SEP 11 2015

CENTRAL LIBRARY
905-884-9288

Available September 2015

Freedom Is Your Only Choice

108 Questions To Discover Your True Self

Ajay Kapoor

Ajay Kapoor's retreats are attended by spiritual seekers from all over the world. *Freedom Is Your Only Choice*, the sequel to his previous book *Free Your Mind*, collects their deepest and most sincere questions related to the common issues that all of us — meditators or non-meditators — face in life, especially on how to attain freedom from our restlessness and pain. Presented in a reader-friendly format, Ajay Kapoor shares his insights on each question and gives answers meaningful for both beginning and advance meditators.

"... goes beyond today's fashionable mindfulness movement by using our thinking, rather than simply noting it. Kapoor carefully shows us how to use our minds to break down our mental conditioning and become truly free."

—Franz Metcalf, author of *What Would Buddha Do?*

$16.95 · ISBN 9781611250428

Celebrating the sacred in everyday life.

Divine Arts was founded to share some of the new and ancient knowledge that is rapidly emerging from the scientific, indigenous, and wisdom cultures of the world, and to present new voices that express eternal truths in innovative, accessible ways.

Although the Earth appears to be in a dark state of affairs, we have realized from the shifts in our own consciousness that millions of beings are seeking and finding a new and optimistic understanding of the nature of reality; and we are committed to sharing their evolving insights.

Our esteemed authors, masters and teachers from around the world, have come together from all spiritual practices to create Divine Arts books. Our unity comes in celebrating the sacredness of life and in having the intention that our work will assist in raising human consciousness and benefiting all sentient beings.

We trust that our work will serve you,
and we welcome your feedback.

Michael Wiese, *publisher*

DIVINE ARTS | DIVINEARTSMEDIA.COM